SOBER MOM

SOBER MOM

A MEMOIR

ELIZABETH JANNUZZI

SHE WRITES PRESS

Published in 2026 by
She Writes Press, an imprint of The Stable Book Group

1569 Solano Ave #546
Berkeley, CA 94707
https://shewritespress.com

Library of Congress Control Number: 2026904372
ISBN: 979-8-89636-348-4
eISBN: 979-8-89636-349-1

Interior designer: Katherine Lloyd, The DESK

Printed in the United States

Names and identifying characteristics have been changed to protect the privacy of certain individuals.

For Chris,
Without you, none of this would be possible.
We have built a beautiful life together.
Let's not fuck it up again.

"Each day, somewhere in the world, recovery begins when one alcoholic talks with another alcoholic, sharing experience, strength, and hope."

—Foreword to the Third Edition,
Alcoholics Anonymous (aka the "Big Book")

WHAT IT WAS LIKE . . .

WHAT IT WAS LIKE . . .

WHAT IT WAS LIKE . . .

WHAT IT WAS LIKE . . .

WHAT IT WAS LIKE . . .

ANY GIVEN NIGHT (IN THE PAST)

The mood in the minivan is jubilant. In the rearview mirror, I see Julia's red curls bob up and down as she bounces in her car seat with excitement. I have just announced to the kids that we're getting McDonald's for dinner. Fast food is considered a treat, offered only occasionally. However, "occasionally" seems to be more and more often, especially when their dad, my husband Chris, is away on a business trip.

"Can we play inside on the playground?" Four-year-old Raymond's voice rises in a plea. I pass the parking spots and maneuver into the drive-thru lane.

"Not tonight," I answer, knowing this will bring down the mood a few notches.

"You never let us play inside," my oldest, Michael, accuses me.

"Come on," I say into the rearview mirror. "Let's get our food and go home and watch a movie. It'll be fun!" I try to reboot the previous "mom is the best" sentiment.

"I just have to make one stop on our way home." I glance in the mirror to see if they have any reaction to that bit of information. They do not, of course. They are two, four, and six and are along for any ride that lets them have chicken nuggets and french fries for dinner.

Before we left the house, I double-checked my wallet for the $20 bill. “Cash back?” the machine asked when I swiped my debit card at the grocery store earlier that day. *Yes, please*. This is how I get cash without Chris noticing.

With the kids happily sampling their fries, I make the stop. I can’t go to Spirits Unlimited because I was there two days ago. Tonight, it’s Vingo, a sketchy liquor store on the wrong side of town. I park strategically so that I can see the car through the store’s windows. I hate leaving the kids in the car, but I also don’t want to drag them into the liquor store. I scan the parking lot for potential kidnappers or nosy do-gooders who will call the police on me for child endangerment. I give my usual spiel to the kids: “I’ll be back in five minutes.” More sternly, I say, “Don’t get out. I’m locking the doors.”

As I enter the store, I’m hit with the wheat-y smell of stale beer, an odor that transports me back to my teen and college days and the morning after a rager. The smell is disgusting but conjures up nostalgia for the “good old days” when drinking was a fun social activity. I pretend to scan the shelves, pondering what I’m going to buy. But I know exactly what I want and where it is. A 1.7-liter bottle of Svedka vodka. It costs less than the $20 I have in my wallet. I use cash so Chris won’t see my liquor store purchase on the debit or credit card statements. I glance out the store’s window at the minivan. The kids are fine; still, I want to hurry.

I don’t know when I started to buy only that type of vodka in that size bottle. I prefer Grey Goose but can’t afford it. Or at least not in the quantity I’m buying. I tried a cheaper vodka brand once and had a terrible hangover. Well, worse than usual. The 1.7-liter is a medium-sized bottle. Even though it would save me money, I would never buy a handle of vodka. The large size of a handle is offensive, like a neon sign blaring, “This household needs *a lot* of vodka." Plus, it's too big to hide. A smaller bottle is better. Although I would never buy a pint. That's what alcoholics buy and swig from on their way home from work, throwing the empty bottle out of the car window into the bushes before pulling into their driveways. Normal people buy average-sized bottles.

These thoughts never actually occur to me at the time. To think these thoughts would be to admit I have a problem. Admit I need to stop drinking. I cannot stop. I'm on a conveyor belt in a factory. The conveyor belt goes from kids' outing to the liquor store and home to drink. It's not a choice I make.

As I hand the bottle to the cashier, I scan the countertop, examining bottle openers and scratch-off tickets. I look everywhere but the cashier's face. I don't want to see any judgment in his dark eyes. Maybe he remembers me from last week. Maybe he sees the kids in the minivan and thinks I'm a bad mother. I try to act like I'm buying a bottle of vodka for a dinner party.

"What did you get, Mom?" Michael asks without looking up from his Nintendo DS when I get back in the car. I tuck the bottle into my large purse, grateful that the brown bag hides its contents.

"A bottle of wine." I don't say vodka for fear the kids might tell Chris one day when they drive past Vingo, "That's where Mom buys vodka." Wine is fine, but vodka would set off alarms. Chris knows I enjoy a beer or a glass of wine with dinner. He doesn't know about the vodka.

I feel my nerves begin to settle. Even without taking a sip, the vodka tucked in my purse untwists the spring that has been tightening in my gut all day.

Back at the house, we are a flurry of plates and ketchup. I put on the movie *Cars* and get them set up with dinner around our coffee table in front of the TV. No food in the living room is our house rule, but the kids know that when Dad is away, the rules are flexible.

"Come watch with us, Momma." Two-year-old Julia pats the couch where she wants me to sit. Her face is already smeared with ketchup. On the screen, the voice of Paul Newman is scolding the voice of Owen Wilson for driving too fast.

"I will. Give me a minute."

With the kids preoccupied, I return to the kitchen and take the brown bag out of my purse. I pour a little vodka into a glass and then add some cranberry juice on top. Just a little this time. Not like last night when I passed out on the floor of the boys' room. I take a big gulp and immediately feel a warming tingle. I take another sip. A sunburst of relief blooms. It starts in my gut and then slowly spreads through my body until it reaches my fingertips and toes. All the day's tensions are washed away with those first sips of vodka. The awkwardness I feel around the well-put-together moms at school pickup. The resentment I feel when my part-time administrative assistant work feels demeaning. The stress of taking care of three little kids on my own while my husband is away. The guilt I feel over having had too much to drink the night before. I close my eyes and feel all the day's stressors dissipate from my body. My shoulders drop, and I let out a sigh.

Before I head into the living room, I top off my glass with more vodka. Then, I tuck the bottle behind the coffee maker on the counter.

"What did I miss?" I ask the kids as I join them on our beige Ikea sectional, the one with the washable slipcovers. Now Owen Wilson is trying to woo Bonnie Hunt. Raymond begins explaining every single detail of the movie. He is a carbon copy of Chris as a boy, with thick dark hair and brown eyes. I smile at him as I sip my drink.

When they finish their dinner, I get up to put their dishes in the dishwasher. I also top off my drink. I look around the kitchen and smile. I've got a good life here. Sure, our house is tiny. It's comical how the five of us squeeze around this small square kitchen table for family dinners. But we don't need much. The kids are mostly happy, or at least they are at this moment. Chris and I have our ups and downs, but I love him. I do. I will make sure to show him when he returns from the trip. I know I have been distant with him. I will be better. I don't know why I complain all the time about my job. I'm lucky to have such a flexible schedule that lets me work and stay home with the kids. Things are good.

The loud trill of our landline interrupts my thoughts, and I scowl at the red phone mounted on our kitchen wall. My jaw clenches at the intrusion. I want to be left alone. I glance at the clock. It's six o'clock. It must be Chris calling to say goodnight to the kids. It's nice that he's calling, but I don't feel like talking to anyone right now. He's interrupting my buzz.

"Hi," I say. "How's it going?" Oh my God, is there a slur in my voice?

"The conference is going well, but I miss you guys. It's so hard to be away."

"I'd give anything to get away for a few days." As soon as the words come out of my mouth, I know it's the wrong thing to say, and I can feel his anger flare through the phone line.

"You know this is work, not a vacation, right?"

"I know. I'm sorry."

"Whatever," he sighs. "Can I say goodnight to the kids?"

I pass the phone around, but the kids don't want to stop watching the movie to talk to their dad. Chris is frustrated, and we say curt goodbyes. I pour another drink.

The movie is over. I tell the kids it's time for bed. They groan, and I snap.

"Come on, we had such a good day and night. I took you to the beach and got you McDonald's. But now it's time for bed."

Ray and Julia do as they're told and march their tiny bodies up the stairs. Michael ignores me. His head is bent over the DS, clicking buttons, playing Super Mario Bros. He is not moving.

"That's it," I scream in his face. "You need to start listening to me. You are grounded!" I rip the DS out of his hands.

"Why do I have to go to bed so early? It's not fair!" He thrusts his red face into mine. I hear Julia quietly crying from her bedroom. I yank his arm and drag him up the stairs. He is only six but big for his age, so this isn't an easy task. The next day I will see the bruise on his arm where my fingers squeezed.

We go through the bedtime routine—pjs, teeth brushing, book reading. With each new request, I'm getting angrier and angrier.

"Can I have a glass of water?" Raymond asks and I lose it.

"That's it. Go to bed." And I stomp down the stairs.

Back in the kitchen, I pour myself another drink. Why did I have to lose my patience so quickly? I head down the hall toward the bathroom and stumble. I lean against the wall to steady myself. Oh no, I've had too much to drink. How did this happen again? I didn't mean to get like this again. I have to stop doing this. Tomorrow. I won't do this tomorrow. I promise. I'll be better tomorrow. I'll be more patient with the kids. I'll take them to Chuck E. Cheese to make up for tonight. I will apologize to Chris for our bad phone conversation. And I won't drink as much. But I might as well finish out the night. And I pour myself another drink.

PROLOGUE

I have a disease of perception. Or at least that's what my sponsor tells me. And I know that's what her sponsor tells her. And my sponsor's sponsor's sponsor tells her. All alcoholics suffer from this disease, is my point. This affliction affects the way I interpret reality. What I think to be true may or may not be, depending on my disease's flare-ups.

Here's what I mean: I think the reason my friend has not returned my call is because she's mad at me. What about? I don't know, I'm sure I said something stupid and hurtful. When my friend finally does phone back, she explains she couldn't call sooner because she was at the doctor's office. My perception was wrong. Need one more example? I think I've explained something clearly and pleasantly to my husband Chris when, in reality, I was vague and "had a tone." You get the picture, right?

So, if I have a disease of perception, then how can you, dear reader, trust me to write an accurate account of my life? Well, you cannot, which is to say the story I'm about to tell is my story, as I remember it, perceived by me, the alcoholic with the disease of perception.

Of course, I'm going to do my best to tell the truth.[1] Honesty is the cornerstone of my recovery. If I lie, I drink. If I drink,

I die. So, I tell the truth. Hard stop. But my truth is filtered through my particular Liz lens.

I've told my story many times before. In church basements, while standing at a podium or sitting at a long table, looking out at a sea of faces—some earnest, some distracted. I get sweaty and nervous, worried that my voice will shake, which inevitably makes my voice shake, praying that what comes out of my mouth will be coherent and will help at least one person sitting out there on their folding chair, sipping from their Styrofoam cup of coffee.

That story, the story I have told from the podium, is included in the Appendix of this memoir. You could flip to the back right now, read that, and know the general gist of my recovery. It would probably take you less than ten minutes to read. It's the condensed version. That version hits all the benchmarks to be considered a good Alcoholics Anonymous (AA) story. I drank a lot, quit drinking when my marriage fell apart. To get sober, I found a sponsor, a network, and a home group. To stay sober, I pass on what was freely given to me.

But that's not the whole story because who could tell the whole story in twenty minutes? And even this 280-page book is not the whole story. In order to focus on a theme, I've omitted some bits that weren't vital to the storyline. Maybe I'll write another memoir about those parts of my life. Maybe not.

All of this is to say, I've done my best with my disease of perception handicap to tell the story of my early recovery as I remember it, presenting it in an entertaining way (I hope).

A Word on AA's Eleventh Tradition

Most everyone knows about AA's Twelve Steps, but those outside of AA, "normies" as we drunks call you, may not know that AA also has a set of "Traditions." AA states: "The Twelve Traditions provide guidelines for relationships between the groups, members, the global Fellowship and society at large."[2]

In general, I agree with the traditions, except for Tradition Eleven, which is: "Our public relations policy is based on attraction rather than promotion; *we need always maintain personal anonymity at the level of press, radio, and films.*" (Emphasis added.)

I'm breaking my anonymity on a public level here by publishing this memoir. I'm openly saying AA got me sober and I'm currently an active member of AA. AA's fear is that if I tell everyone about getting sober with AA and then I drink again (in the rooms of AA, we call it "go out" or "pick up"), then you regular people will say, "See? AA doesn't work!"

I may relapse. It is certainly possible. It's a "one day at a time" program. However, I believe, due to a shift in public awareness, that most people have a deeper understanding of addiction and alcoholism and AA's involvement in recovery. Yes, AA can help someone get sober, but alcoholism is a motherfucker and people will and do relapse, people both in and outside of a twelve-step program. Relapse doesn't have to be a part of recovery, but it often is. What's wonderful about AA is that it's always there to welcome you back if you do "go out."

I don't think anyone should feel ashamed of their disease, whether it be addiction, alcoholism, or mental illness. I feel strongly, as the author Brené Brown does an excellent job of explaining, that normalization is the antidote to shame. I break my anonymity, going against AA's Eleventh Tradition, in order to normalize alcoholism and relieve myself and others of the shame that surrounds addiction.

Ok, have I got all the disclaimers in? Let's get down to it! Do you know what the first assignment is when you begin "working the steps" with your sponsor? It's "Write your story—what it was like, what happened, and what it is like now."

Grab a coffee or tea, preferably not in a Styrofoam cup, sit back, and relax. Try to identify with my story and not compare.

Hi, I'm Liz and I'm an alcoholic.

MY FIRST DRUNK

May 1986
Twenty-five years until sober

The Greyhound bus pulls into the motel parking lot and the entire eighth grade piles out, grabs their bags, and heads toward their assigned rooms. We arrived in Washington, DC, late this morning and have spent the day touring the city. So far, my favorite sites have been the National Mall with the huge Lincoln Memorial on one end and the National Monument on the other.

I am bunking in a room with three other girls. Only one, Cathi, is my good friend. I'm friendly with the other two girls, Jane and Sally, but we aren't super close. If it had been last year, I would've been upset if I hadn't roomed with Susan, my best friend since fourth grade. But for some reason, last year Susan decided she no longer wanted to be my friend. Seventh grade was hard. I cried all the time. I couldn't understand why she stopped calling. But I like hanging out with Cathi. She's funny and easygoing. I still worry that Susan and her new friends are off doing cooler, better things than me. But for this trip, I know I'm doing the coolest thing. As far as I know, I'm the only eighth grader who brought stuff to drink.

I gathered the liquor from several different sources. In a glass Ball jar, I snuck pours from the crystal decanters of the people I babysat for and from my mother's Dewar's Scotch that sits in the cupboard in our kitchen. A little from here, a little from there. Eventually, I had an almost full jar. I kept it in the trunk in my room until our trip to DC. Then, I slipped a white tube sock over the full Ball jar and packed it underneath my underwear in my overnight bag. Luckily, no one searched our bags.

"Good night, girls," the chaperone says as she peeks her head in to make sure we are all there and accounted for.

"Good night!" We respond in unison, like the orphan girls from *Annie*. We have no intention of going to bed. The night is just starting. The chaperone leaves and we all jump around the room with excitement.

"Did you get the ice?" Jane asks. She and Sally are planning on piercing a third hole in their ears. Not me. I'm going to crack open the Ball jar.

"Who wants a drink?" I say, holding up the amber-colored liquid. The other girls shrug their shoulders. We've been planning this night for weeks, but now no one seems excited to drink. I twist the metal cap off the jar and gag from the smell.

Why do people like this stuff, I wonder. Why does my mom drink it every night? Why do my sisters and brother keep having parties and getting drunk whenever my parents are out of town? I'm about to find out. I take a tiny sip. It's awful, disgusting, and it's all I can do not to run to the bathroom to spit it in the sink. I force the swallow down and wait.

"Cathi, do you want some?"

"Sure," she says. "I'll try it." She flicks back her straight brown hair and grabs the jar. She brings the glass to her mouth and slowly tips it so that the brown liquid barely reaches her lips. Her face grimaces, flashing a mouthful of silver braces.

"Ew, it's gross," she says and hands it back to me quickly. I take another sip, slightly bigger than the first. It's a little easier to get down the second time. I start to feel something. A warm glow inside my body.

I take the jar to the bathroom, where Jane is sitting on the toilet, holding an ice cube up to her left ear. Sally is pouring rubbing alcohol on a safety pin.

"Do you want a sip?" I ask. They both shake their heads. Sally sticks the safety pin in Jane's earlobe.

"Take it out! We didn't numb it long enough," Jane screams.

It's approaching midnight and we are all hyped up, running from the bathroom to the beds and back again. The Saturday Night Movie is on TV, but no one is watching it. The room is electric, and I feel so close to these girls. I'm the only one taking sips from the Ball jar but that doesn't seem to matter.

"Should we play Light as a Feather or MASH?" I ask.

"MASH will say you will marry John," Sally teases me.

"Well, you want to marry Timmy!" I respond and give her a push on the bed. There is a loud knock on the door, and we all freeze. I glance around for the Ball jar. It's out in the open on the dresser next to the TV. My heart clenches in fear. If the chaperone comes in and sees it, we are screwed. But through the door, the chaperone says, "Quiet down, girls. Lights off!"

"Ok, we will," Cathi speaks through the door as Jane, Sally, and I clamp our hands over our mouths to suppress our giggles, and roll around the bed.

When I'm confident the chaperone has moved down the hall, I bring the Ball jar to the bathroom and pour the contents down the sink. I'm feeling woozy, and the smell of the liquor wafting up from the sink makes my stomach queasy. I lean over the toilet and vomit.

The next morning, we tour the United States Mint. Our tour guide is droning on and on about coin production and the Department of the Treasury. We are herded through the factory where the metal is dyed and the coins are cut and polished. There is a horrible smell, and I feel nauseous. I am dizzy and sweaty, and I need to lean up against the wall to steady myself. My classmates squeeze past me to follow the tour. I've heard my sisters talk about hangovers and I've seen them on TV. There is an episode of *Moonlighting* in which David Addison is hungover and puts an ice pack on his head. I wish I had an ice pack now to help me get through this tour.

On the bus ride home to New Jersey, I opt to sit by myself and attempt to sleep stretched out across two seats. I don't feel like talking to anyone. The camaraderie I felt last night with my roommates has vanished. I'm worried Cathi is mad at me. She seems distant. But also, everyone is annoying me. I'm grateful when I see my mom's station wagon waiting for me in the school's parking lot.

"How was your trip?" my mother asks.

"It was good, I guess. The bus ride made me feel sick."

When we arrive home, I go straight to bed. The next time I babysit, I swipe a bottle of red wine.

LITTLE PINK HOUSES

December 6, 2010, Part 1
Thirty-three days until sober

It's midday on a Monday in December and I'm holed up in my first-floor bedroom, while outside the bedroom door electricians are milling about. They are here to complete the final tasks of our house renovation. We're expanding our small Cape Cod, adding a bathroom on the second floor and bumping out the kids' bedrooms with dormer windows. It's a typical expansion for our central New Jersey suburban neighborhood where we've lived for three years.

Every time I drive around our town, I'm reminded of a lyric from a John Mellencamp song about pink houses. Of course, the houses in our neighborhood are not pink. Ours is white with sky blue shutters. But there is something so American about these tiny box Capes constructed in the 1950s, carbon copies of each other evenly spaced on a grid of grass lots and roads. There is also something so depressing about them. The aluminum siding, the chain-link fences protecting yards littered with dog poop and broken toys. It's like seeing failed dreams, one after another after another. Sometimes, when I walk around our neighborhood, I ponder: *How did we end up here? How did I end up here?*

I know the answer, of course. When I became pregnant with Julia and our family was growing from four to five, we could no longer fit in the tiny crooked house on Huntington Bay, Long Island that we rented from Chris's sister. When Chris agreed to look at houses in New Jersey, I was ecstatic at the chance to move back to my home state. We'd be closer to my parents. Closer to my sister and her three kids. The kids would have instant playmates! I wanted to move away from Huntington and our troubles there. I wanted to come home. *Things will get better when we move to New Jersey*, I remember thinking.

As a result, I had blinders on when it came to choosing a house we could afford. I saw this cute Cape as a perfect starter home. I didn't notice the surrounding area. I didn't see the neighborhood's desperation until I became the one desperate in it.

Renovating the house seems to be Chris's answer to fixing our problems. We just need more space. The kids need their own bathroom. Things will get better when the kids have their own bathroom.

I have no idea how we are able to afford this renovation. According to Chris, we are always broke, and I get scolded for spending too much money on groceries.

Chris is an executive director at the College Board, a nonprofit membership organization. I used to work there too, as a senior editor of its website. That's where we met. After we married, I left that job for another. Then I got pregnant and then I got laid off. When our firstborn son Michael was a baby, I would babysit to make ends meet. But then our son Raymond came along two years later and babysitting with a toddler and a newborn in tow was too difficult. Just before our daughter Julia was born, my father offered me a job as his administrative assistant.

If I can separate feeling like a failure because I "work for my dad" and many of my job responsibilities can feel demeaning, like changing light bulbs, I can see that this part-time job is a win-win solution. My father, a seventy-two-year-old retired federal judge, needs administrative help with his growing arbitration business. I need to feel like I'm doing something besides changing diapers and packing lunches. Also, while at work, I get to check in on my seventy-one-year-old mother. Her health has been on a slow decline for almost a decade, but lately the hill has tilted sharply, and now her health is rapidly failing. More often than not, because my father is busy with his arbitration work, I'm the one who takes my mother to her doctor's appointments. I'm grateful that my job allows for that.

Plus, the extra money helps. Although I guess it's not enough. Every month, when Chris goes through the bills, he grumbles about one expense or the other.

Somehow, though, Chris was able to secure financing for this house renovation. He orchestrated the whole construction project, from the architect's plans to choosing a contractor. When I can, I avoid the construction workers—the carpenters, the plumbers, the tile guys. I'm so uncomfortable around them. If they are not leering at me in a creepy way, they are talking down to me, expecting me to understand how a toilet works or to know the exact measurements of a room. I try to hand off all direct communications with the construction guys to Chris. But of course Chris is the one with the full-time job. I'm the one mostly at home during the day.

Currently, Chris is away on a business trip. San Francisco, or is it San Diego? He is always traveling somewhere for some conference.

As coworkers, before we were married, we'd travel on these work trips together. Indianapolis, Orlando, San Diego, Las Vegas,

Savannah. These are the cities where we fell in love. During the day, we'd have booth duty in the exhibit hall, where we'd promote our company's website to high school counselors. At night, Chris would plan some fun adventure for anyone who was game. A trip to a haunted corn maze in Indianapolis. A tour of the Hoover Dam in Las Vegas. A road trip to find the best BBQ in Austin, Texas. Oh, how I loved these mini adventures! With each trip, I fell more in love.

"Gregarious" was how my company's newsletter described Chris in the announcement of his hire. It sounds like a cliché, but he was different from the normal guys I dated. First off, he looked different. Of Italian descent, he had long graying hair (even though he wasn't thirty yet) that he would pull back in a ponytail. I usually went for baseball-capped preppy types. Like a Renaissance man, Chris played guitar, spoke fluent German, and watched indie films. I was smitten after we staffed our first booth together in April 1998 at the Hilton on Sixth Avenue in New York City. On that day, we were both tired and dragging at work, but for very different reasons. He had pulled an all-nighter, gambling with his friends in Atlantic City. I was limping around the conference center because I had run the Jersey Shore Marathon the previous day. If you were to judge us on that day, you might think I was the put-together one, the Type A personality, a marathon runner. Chris you'd see as the wild one, having drunk and gambled the night away. But oh, how wrong that impression would be. Typically, I was the one to show up to work hungover.

That was twelve years ago. Now we've been married nine years and are living in this grid of Cape houses with our three kids: rambunctious Michael, age seven with curly auburn hair and my hazel eyes; sweet Raymond, age five with dark brown hair and eyes; and almost-three-year-old Julia with red hair, large brown eyes, and Chris's wide smile.

At the moment, the boys are at school, Michael in first grade and Raymond in preschool. Julia is upstairs napping. I should be using this free time to book my boss's/father's flight to Paris. But instead, while the electricians are installing smoke detectors outside my bedroom door, I am sitting at my Ikea desk sipping a vodka cranberry and crafting yet another email to Bob, the man with whom I had a one-night affair in October.

SISTER CHRISTIAN

October 8–11, 1998
Thirteen years until sober

I step out of the shower onto the generic beige tile of the hotel bathroom. This Westin bathroom is ridiculously large, and the space feels luxurious compared to my tiny New York City apartment bathroom. I wipe the steam off the mirror and look at my face. About a month ago, I broke out in a weird skin rash. A type of acne, said the dermatologist, but it felt like a rash to me. Little red bumps spread across my back and then up my neck and then, much to my horror, up and across my face. I was mortified. How can I still be breaking out at age twenty-six? At the peak of the inflammation, when my face was covered in little red bumps, I ran into John, an old high school crush, on the train from New York to Red Bank. It was late Saturday morning, and the train was empty. He flipped the seat over with a *bang*, creating a six-seater booth so that he could sit across from me. Any other time I might've been thrilled to have John stop and talk to me, but instead I felt incredibly awkward. Because of the rash, but also because of my sister Julia's death, which now complicated any interaction I had with people from my hometown.

Anytime I run into a former classmate or a resident from Fair Haven, the town where I grew up, I panic that the person will bring up Julia and I'll have to explain all that's happened in the past two years. The failed suicide attempt, the coma, the surgeries, the long stays in different hospitals, and why she never recovered. I am terrified they'll ask, "What happened?" because I don't know.

I don't know why Julia swallowed the pills. I don't know if she really meant to kill herself or if it was just a cry for help. I don't know if she might have survived after she woke up from the coma, if she hadn't aspirated the chicken dinner the doctor told her to eat. I don't know if that regurgitated chicken dinner getting stuck in her airway caused permanent brain damage. I don't know why my parents never pursued a lawsuit for negligence against the hospital. I don't know why her body continued to fail, her large colon breaking open, spilling shit into her insides, causing sepsis. I don't know why the surgeries for the sepsis didn't fully heal her. Or why she kept getting transferred from rehabilitation center to rehabilitation center without anyone really saying what was wrong with her. I don't know why, when I spoon-fed her applesauce, the sauce seeped out of the tracheotomy hole in her neck. I don't know why, after she attempted to kill herself, God let her live for eight more months before killing her.

When I bump into acquaintances, I avoid discussing any of this. I babble about trivial things like the weather or my job so they can't get a word in. Then I end the conversation abruptly and bolt. But after these interactions are over, I'm left feeling empty and mildly upset. Why did they not mention Julia? I don't want to discuss her death, but I don't want Julia to be forgotten either. It's complicated. It's easier to be around people who don't know that I had a brother who died in a car crash and a sister who died by suicide.

"I broke out in a rash all over my face," I mumbled to John when I bumped into him on the train.

"I don't see it," he replied, his ice-blue eyes meeting mine, causing me to glance away and stare out the window at the landscape whizzing past. I usually see this guy in Brannigan's, a hole-in-the-wall local bar. In the bar, with a beer in my hand and one foot resting on the rail, I can make eye contact and small talk. On the train, I was sober with a rash and a dead sister and brother. I didn't know what to say or where to look.

"Can you lend me five dollars?" he asked. Oh, so that's why he stopped to chat. I gave him the money and he moved on to another car. When I got off at our stop, I didn't look around for him at the station. I just put my rashy head down and jumped into a waiting cab.

Now, in this steamy Westin bathroom, I think about this embarrassing exchange as I examine my face in the mirror, looking for signs of the rash. It has cleared up thanks to the cream the dermatologist gave me. And for once I'm not totally distraught about what I see in the mirror. The red bumps are gone and for some reason I don't have the usual dark circles under my eyes. Being in this hotel room is good for my complexion. It's good for my mental state as well.

I was glad when my boss, Mary Carroll, told me I was to attend NACAC, the National Association of College Admission Counseling, a four-day conference in Indianapolis. My main duty was to man the College Board booth in the exhibit hall. I didn't care what I had to do. I was happy to get away. Lately, all I've been doing is following my roommate Kelly and her boyfriend Scott around. I went out to dinner with them. I went to MOMA with them. I went to concerts in Central Park with them. They graciously invite me to every event, but I'm starting to feel like maybe they don't want my company on every date. The nights that I decline their invitation to be a third wheel, all I do is drink alone in the apartment. I buy a six-pack of Sierra Nevada from the bodega on the corner and spend the night drinking and watching TV or listening to sad songs on my Walkman and crying. One night recently, after drinking four beers, I switched to white wine. We had more than half a bottle left over from a dinner party. I finished the bottle and ended up passing out on our apartment's couch. The next morning, Kelly said she repeatedly tried to wake me up to go to bed but I wouldn't wake up. Her tone was matter-of-fact, nonjudgmental, but I was embarrassed and ashamed to be seen like that. I brushed it off with, "Oh yeah, I was so tired."

I often go to my parents' house in New Jersey for the weekend. There I can drink until I pass out and no one will notice. But it's difficult to be home. Especially since it's October, the two-year anniversary of when Julia swallowed the five bottles of antidepressants and went into a coma. The calendar in general is something to avoid. June 13th, the day Julia died. August 10th, the day my brother William died. Easter, Thanksgiving, and Christmas—holidays at which we pretend to be happy but the pain and grief we never talk about or address hovers in the air, mingling with the smell of a roasting turkey.

When I'm at home, I drink my mom's scotch. There's always a large handle of it in the liquor cabinet. I can't stomach the stuff straight up, so I mix it with cider or orange juice. I take my drink and wander through the large empty house. I think about the epic games of hide-and-seek we had. Or summer nights when our Monopoly games seemed to go on forever. Or how Julia would insist that I watch scary movies with her, *Poltergeist* or *The Shining*. She loved horror films, but I wouldn't sleep for days. I wonder how it all went to shit. How our happy childhood ended in death. My parents have been talking about selling the house. My sister Roseann is upset, wishing she could somehow scrounge up the money to buy it herself. Although I do love the house, I have no feelings one way or the other about them selling it. I am numb.

Getting out of Dodge with a four-day trip to Indianapolis seemed like the perfect solution. I don't want to think about the house, or Julia, or that soon my roommate Kelly will get engaged and I can't seem to find a boyfriend, or one that doesn't suck.

I bend over so my long, wet hair hangs down and I wrap it up in a thick white towel, twisting the towel like a turban on my head. Then I take another towel, wrap it around my body, and head out of the bathroom. I pass the room service tray next to the door. Last night I ordered a grilled chicken sandwich and one beer. One drink, like a civilized adult. But of course, after drinking the beer, I wanted more. I knew I couldn't hit the minibar; I don't want that showing up on my expense report. But the one beer was unsatisfying. I thought about heading down to the hotel bar, but a woman going to a bar by herself? Too pathetic. I went to bed after that one beer and this morning I'm relieved I didn't drink more, and I feel great.

After drying off, I get dressed in the hotel room, which goes more smoothly than when I get dressed in my apartment. There's no hemming or hawing about what to wear, going from my closet to Kelly's closet and back again. I already have an outfit picked and there is no other choice. It's my typical office wear: black Gap pants, black leather boots, and a sweater. I review the outfit in the mirror and feel I'm presentable enough for booth duty. My hair has dried into long, wavy blonde curls and for once I feel like I look pretty.

I find the exhibit hall and the College Board booth. My boss, Mary Carroll, is there. She is in a good mood, flitting here and there with her colleagues. This is her element. She feels important. I used to think she was very important, but now I know that's not true. She is divorced and her children are college age. She spends most of her time at the office not because she has so much to do but because she has no one to go home to. The problem is she expects her underlings to do the same.

"There's a great session today," she tells me. "'Practical Implications for the 2007–8 FAFSA on Admission and Enrollment Management Offices.' When the exhibit hall closes, you should come," suggests Mary Carroll.

"Oh yes, that does sound interesting," I lie. "I'll see . . ."

When I first started working these conferences, I did attend the sessions, eagerly taking notes and thinking I could apply what I learned to my job as website content provider. But I've been at the College Board for almost a year now and I know that it's all a bunch of bullshit. Nothing ever changes, and if it does, it certainly isn't because of something I've said in a meeting. The sessions are a waste of time. This whole conference is just an excuse for people to escape from their lives for a couple of days.

Mary Carroll rushes off and I plant myself at the booth. Our table is set up with placards promoting SAT Online Registration and our College and Scholarship searches. Several computers are logged on to our home page. My job is to encourage interested parties to tour the website, and to show them our College Search. The first time I had booth duty I was a nervous wreck. But now I know the drill: smile at passersby, lure them to our table with free mousepads, and encourage them to check out our website. I've helped create the student side of the website and worked extensively on its College Search, so I'm comfortable talking to people about it.

An hour goes by and not much is happening. I'm organizing the mousepads when I hear:

"Excuse me, miss. Can you please explain why *my* college doesn't appear on the top of your College Search results?"

I turn, expecting to face an angry admissions officer, but instead I see it's Chris.

"How's it going?" asks Chris, placing his computer bag down under the table.

"It was busy earlier, but things have slowed down now. Everyone must be in a session," I answer.

"A bunch of tools retooling the future," he says, making fun of the conference's tagline, "Retooling and Refueling Our Future."

"Or refueling with a liquid lunch," says Jane. "You know Mary Carroll is!"

"Has she been by?" Chris asks.

"Yes." I roll my eyes. "She's busy, busy, busy."

Chris and Jane plop themselves on the stools at the booth. I'm grateful to have company, especially Chris. He opens the paper he has been holding.

"We are thinking of going to a haunted corn maze tonight," he says while scanning through the paper. "Do you want to come?"

"Come with us," says Jane. "It'll be fun."

"You have a car?" I ask.

"Yup, I rented one," says Chris. "I usually do on these trips."

"So you can hit the casinos." Jane pushes his arm with a laugh. Jane has an uncanny resemblance to Elaine from Seinfeld and in this moment is even acting like her.

I wonder what the deal is with Jane and Chris. I don't think they are dating but they seem awfully chummy.

I agree to go, and we make a plan to meet at the hotel bar at 5:30 p.m.

What does one wear to a haunted corn maze? I wonder. I didn't pack many outfits. I wasn't planning on going out after booth duty. I put on a pair of jeans and a sweater and I'm happy with the result. I look nice but not like I'm trying too hard.

I arrive at the hotel bar and look at my watch: 5:20 p.m. I'm early as usual. But that's okay because I can order a beer. A woman at the bar is not pathetic if she is waiting for someone. I drink half my beer before Chris and Jane arrive. They come together, which makes me wonder.

"Let's go," says Chris, and I'm a little taken aback that they don't want to have a drink before we go. I finish my beer in one long gulp and then stand up. I notice Chris checking me out.

"Do you hear the song?" I point at the speakers in the ceiling.

"'Sister Christian,' a classic!" I've earned some points with Chris and Jane for ironically liking an old pop song. The truth is I really like it.

When we get to the car in the hotel's garage, I quickly stake out my spot in the back. I don't want to sit up front and feel pressure to talk. I'm good in the back seat, in the background. On our way out of downtown Indianapolis we stop to get gas and, much to my relief, Jane comes out of the convenience store with a six-pack of bottled beer.

Chris doesn't seem thrilled, but Jane assures him that they don't have open container laws in Indiana. I'm not sure that's true but I'm not questioning it. Jane takes a beer out of the cardboard sleeve and hands the six-pack back to me. I take one too and then put it on the floor.

Jane is in charge of reading Chris the directions to the corn maze from the ad in the paper. I sit in the back and listen to them talk. They talk about bands I never heard of and art exhibits. They seem so artistic and intellectual, so "city." I feel like an out-of-touch bridge and tunnel girl, even though I actually live in Manhattan, while Chris lives in Long Island and Jane in Jersey City.

I finish one beer and desperately want another one. But Jane had one and is apparently done. I don't want to seem like a lush, so I don't take another one.

"Build Me Up Buttercup" comes on the radio and we all sing along as if we were at karaoke. I sing loudly. Chris looks at me in the rearview mirror, his large, brown, almond-shaped eyes twinkling.

"Wow, you know all the words!" he says, impressed.

"One of my favorites," I admit. I don't tell him the song reminds me of my old boyfriend John who, like the song says, would never call, *baby*, when he said he would. I'm warmed by the attention from Chris.

After a forty-five-minute drive, we find the corn maze. The place is packed. It must be a big attraction. Parking attendants dressed in yellow vests motion to tell us where to park even though it's obvious where we should go.

"Here? We should go here," Chris says to the parking attendants and parks off to the side, not where they had wanted us to go. The young guys glare at us, which makes me uncomfortable, but Chris and Jane are laughing.

"I'll go buy our tickets," Chris says. "I'll be right back."

"Don't ever say, 'I'll be right back . . .'" I'm referencing the trailer from the hit movie *Scream*.

"What?" Chris gives me a weird look.

"You know, from the movie *Scream*."

"Oh, I never saw it," says Chris.

"He's a movie snob," Jane explains.

"But you've seen the trailer, right?" I ask. "I mean, they play that commercial nonstop."

"I don't really watch TV," Chris replies.

Who is this guy? I start to wonder. Who doesn't watch TV and hasn't seen the movie *Scream*?

Chris goes off to buy the tickets and Jane and I wait by the car.

"Chris is so great. Isn't he?" says Jane. "I always feel safe around him."

When Chris comes back, we walk across the mowed hay field to the maze entrance. It is dark but the whole area is lit up by spotlights. We are greeted by a vampire.

"You all from around here?" asks Dracula.

"Ah no," replies Jane. "We are from New York."

When we are out of earshot of the vampire, Jane says, "Can't he tell we are not from around here? I mean, don't we smell like we are from New York?" She sounds elitist and I can tell this comment annoys Chris, although he doesn't say anything. I don't think they are dating.

We make our way through the maze. Chris is in the lead, then Jane, and then me. Chris stops abruptly.

"Turn around," he says. "This is a dead end."

I turn and come face-to-face with a black-hooded ghoul holding a machete who has been quietly walking behind me for several minutes. My heart leaps out of my chest and an uncontrollable blood-curdling shriek comes from deep within. I frantically step backwards and in doing so I fall and land on my butt. I'm literally scared off my feet. The ghoul takes off and we all start laughing. I can't believe how scared I was. Chris gives me a hand and helps me up and I wipe the dirt and hay off my jeans. I'm surprised that I got so scared and also that I'm having a great time. Another freakish-looking dude comes running at us with a chainsaw. The chainsaw is loud and I can't believe they would allow something so dangerous. Later, I realize there was no chain in the chainsaw. Jane and I stay close behind Chris and we eventually make it out of the maze.

"That was so fun," I say to Chris. "Thanks for the idea."

Back at the car, Jane insists I sit up front so that she can sleep in the back.

"Do you need me to reverse the directions to go back to the hotel?" I ask.

"We are not going home. We are going to a riverboat casino," says Chris.

"What? Really?" I say. "Okay, I'm game." I'm energized from the fright fest. Jane makes a few feeble protests from the back seat, but Chris won't listen. We are going gambling. I know there are still four beers left in the car but neither Jane nor Chris makes a move to drink one, so I don't either.

Chris and I chitchat on the way to the casino riverboat while Jane sleeps in the back. Chris tells me he is the youngest of seven in a large, Italian family. His grandfather was a partier, gambler, and drinker, and Chris is going to invoke his spirit at the craps table. At one point on the drive, we get a little lost and end up in Ohio.

"This is crazy," I laugh. "Where are we?" But I don't mind the detour. I'm enjoying the conversation and Chris's company. And best of all, when we finally get there, I invoke the spirit of my gambling grandmother and win $300 on the slot machines. On the way home, I offer to pay for everyone's meal. We pass a White Castle and when Chris learns I have never been to one, he insists we go and turns the car around.

Back in the office in New York, Chris begins to make regular stops at my desk. In the mornings he comes by and we take the elevator together to the second-floor kitchen for coffee and a bagel. Before heading back to our desks, we talk a while by the elevator banks, taking sips of our coffee from Styrofoam cups. Then we start going to lunch together at a nearby diner. He gets a cup of soup and we split a turkey sandwich. Sometimes, after work, we go to happy hour for half-priced margaritas at Rosa Mexicano, across from Lincoln Center. But he never stays for more than one drink. We talk about work, making fun of Mary Carroll and her cohorts. We talk about funny movies, his favorite being *The Big Lebowski*. We talk about our childhoods.

He tells me funny stories about his family. But he never talks much about what he does after work and on the weekends. And I never talk about William or Julia or the calendar and its constant reminder of death.

One day, in mid-November, we are walking along Columbus Avenue, heading back to the office after a Starbucks run. I ask him about his plans for Thanksgiving, knowing that he doesn't really want to tell me.

"I'm having dinner with my girlfriend's family," he answers. His tone has changed; his shoulders slump and he is staring at the sidewalk.

An awkwardness hangs in the air. He's admitted it. Said it out loud. Explained to me the situation. That he and I are only friends. But by then it's too late. I've fallen in love.

WRECKING BALL

December 6, 2010, Part 2
Thirty-three days until sober

The electrician knocks on my bedroom door. He needs to install the new smoke detectors on the ceiling.

"Go ahead," I say. I mean to convey an easy breezy tone but for some reason it comes out snarky. My vodka cranberry sits next to my laptop. He is two feet away from me, arms stretched over his head, tools hanging off his belt. Can he smell the vodka? Usually I go to great lengths to hide my drinking, but the construction men are taking too long, and I couldn't wait any longer to soothe my nerves. Is it my imagination or did the electrician sneer at me?

The email I am writing to Bob as the sound of electric screwdrivers buzzes around my house reiterates what I've already said to him several times before in texts and emails: that I can't believe he has totally cut me off after our one night together in October. Even though that's what we both agreed would happen when we started flirting online back in June, I wasn't prepared for the abruptness of the end. I was shocked by the return of the loneliness. My Blackberry, which was once a source of delight and adventure, now makes me feel dejected, empty. I keep thinking that if I can just explain things better, explain my feelings more clearly, he will understand and contact me. We will continue with our daily flirtatious text exchanges. Doesn't he know that I am not planning on leaving Chris, that I know what we have (or had) is just temporary? I just don't understand why it has to end as if we've driven off a cliff. Can't we keep it going until the car eventually runs out of gas?

I started seeing a therapist a few weeks ago, after I plummeted into a depression when the affair came to its abrupt end. With short hair and glasses, Dr. Michelle Rabinowitz is a no-nonsense, plain-Jane type. She said people have affairs because they are unhappy in their life.

"It's a Band-Aid," she explained.

My affair with Bob began shortly after our fifteenth college reunion at the end of June. After reconnecting at the reunion party, we exchanged a series of Facebook messages which led to Yahoo messenger texts. He lives several states away, so for a while it was just flirty texts and occasional awkward phone calls. But then we crafted a plan to meet up—one night at a Marriott in Hartford, CT. He had a work trip, and I concocted a fake girls' weekend. I would meet him there. A few days before the planned tryst, my interest waned. Our text exchanges had lost some of their sparkle. I was ready to call the whole thing off. I should have called the whole thing off. But I felt like I couldn't. I was on a moving walkway, like the ones they have at the airport, and I couldn't find a way to escape. I moved forward with the plan. If only I had found the emergency stop button.

Bob completely cut me off immediately after I left the hotel room the morning after our one night. I sent him laboriously crafted, sickly-sweet texts and I got radio silence in return. Getting cut off has made my life topsy-turvy. I feel unmoored. How can I get dumped if I'm married? And although I don't want to leave Chris for Bob, I miss that crutch that helped me get through the day. I got used to the mood boost I'd receive from the ding of my Blackberry. Now that the texts have stopped, I feel like I've fallen into a pit of quicksand. I'm slowly sinking deeper into a depression. I have no idea how to get through the day, the weeks, the years. I've started drinking earlier and earlier in the day. Part of me knows I'm incapable of quitting drinking, although I wouldn't admit this to myself. I wish I drank like a normal housewife, a glass or two of wine while I prep dinner. Instead I'm slugging back vodka cranberries as soon as my coffee buzz wears off in the morning. But that's not why I see Dr. Rabinowitz.

"Please tell me what I have to do to be happy," I beg her. I don't tell her about drinking vodka during the day. I've never told any therapist how much I drink. Why would I? Drinking is not the problem. My job is the problem; I have no career. Chris is the problem; our marriage is failing. My parents are the problem; they didn't love me enough. My life is the problem.

The electrician finishes with the smoke detectors and leaves my bedroom just as the contractor, Christian, pops his head in. Despite his tattoos and piercings, Christian is quiet and kind—an exception to my all-construction-guys-are-jerks theory. I never get the sense he's judging me or leering at me. Christian reports that he is done for the day. He'll be back tomorrow to install the molding in the upstairs bathroom and then he's finished. I thank him and he and the other men leave.

The house and I sigh with relief when they pull out of the driveway. I relish the quiet. I reread my email to Bob but suddenly I'm very sleepy. Julia will probably be asleep for another forty minutes and I have an hour before I pick the boys up from school. I leave the cursor blinking on the Dear Bob email and head over to my bed, taking my drink with me. I just need to close my eyes for a few minutes.

A loud ringing wakes me up. It's our landline phone. My

eyes jerk open and immediately land on my almost-empty drink. The glass is dirty with my fingerprints and precariously placed on my dusty nightstand, shoved between my digital alarm clock and a paperback I've been meaning to read. The glass was once full—half cheerful, bright red cranberry juice and half vodka. But there is only a sad sip of pinkish backwash left.

The clock reads 2:12 p.m. Frantic, I jump out of bed, knocking over the paperback. How long have I been asleep? I physically shake my head to remove the fog from my brain. *What day is it? Where are the kids?* My mind slowly focuses. That's right. Julia is napping; she's probably ready to wake up. And the boys are at school. I sit back down on the side of my unmade bed. The phone rings four times before the answering machine picks up. The caller hangs up without leaving a message. *Telemarketer*, I think. While still sitting on the bed, I stare into the mirror on my closet door. I'm in jeans and a long-sleeved T-shirt. My ponytail has come loose during my nap, and I raise my arms to pull it back tight into the elastic. When I do, my shirt lifts and I can see my belly fat and the roll of extra skin that developed after having three C-sections. Disgusted, I pull my shirt down. I walk past the laptop with the email and go to the bathroom to splash water on my face and brush my teeth.

I head towards the kitchen to brew a pot of coffee and the phone rings again. Alarm bells go off in my head. Something is wrong. My realization begins to bloom. Time slows and I can sense the wrecking ball swinging on its chain from the crane. First it swings back and then, like a pendulum, it reverses its course straight for me. *Wham*, I'm hit with the knowledge of what's happening. Of the mistake I've made. I turn on my heels and run into the bedroom where the laptop is.

I left the email on the computer screen when I went to take a nap. Let's face it, when I passed out. I didn't delete it or hide it in a drafts folder. I just left it on the screen as if it were a shopping list or my boss's/dad's travel itinerary. Chris, who is away on a business trip, has access to our laptop. We use software that allows us to connect to our computer remotely. At least once a day, Chris logs on to our home computer to do the budget or grab a family photo. I look at the computer and there is a Microsoft Notepad message up on the screen covering up my email to Bob.

"I guess we need to talk, Liz."

My stomach drops and the vodka cranberry lurches up in my throat. I quickly shut down the computer so that I can think. The phone rings again and I answer it. It's Chris.

"What the hell is going on, Liz?"

"I don't want to talk about it now. I need to pick up the kids soon. We will talk about it when you get home." Delay is my only tactic.

"No, I want answers . . ."

"Not now," I cut him off and hang up the phone.

Fuck, fuck, fuck. I'm screwed. I run back and forth from the kitchen to the bedroom. I want to turn on the computer to erase any evidence, but if I do, Chris might jump on it. But he's already seen the email so there is no hiding anything now. My heart pounds and the blood rushes to my face. I grab my glass from the nightstand and rinse it out in the sink. Without thinking, I grab the vodka that's hidden behind the Cuisinart blender, pour it into the glass, and top it off with cranberry juice. The drink is strong, and the vodka stings a bit before going down my throat. It lands in my stomach with a familiar and welcoming warmth. I feel the effects immediately. My body loosens. My shoulders drop and I unclench my hands, stretch out my fingers. When I breathe out, I realize I had been holding my breath. I stare out the kitchen window at the weeds in our gravel driveway and think: *What the fuck am I going to do now?*

SIN WILL FIND YOU OUT

"I got drunk at the office Christmas party and ended up in a house in Jersey with a wife and three kids."

—Chris

December 1998
Thirteen years until sober

It's early in the evening on Friday, December 18, 1998. Chris and I are walking down 9th Avenue to my apartment on 51st Street. I have on my wool J.Crew pea coat but I don't really need it. There's a pulse to the city that's warming the air: New York on the verge of the holiday season. You can smell chestnuts roasting from the carts on every other corner. That old holiday song makes it sound like it's a good smell, but it makes me gag whenever we pass through the wafting smoke.

We struggle to walk side by side on the sidewalk as we dodge through the crowd going in the opposite direction, uptown, probably to Lincoln Center to see a show. Chris is not wearing a jacket; his hands are shoved in the pockets of his khakis to keep warm. He has on a black cashmere sweater with a red and black tartan scarf wrapped around his neck. We've just left the College Board's holiday party and are headed to the after-party at my apartment. I planned this event specifically so I could invite Chris. I'm going to make my move tonight, or create an atmosphere so magical that he will make a move. All of our flirting since the October business trip to Indianapolis has led us to this moment and I'm giddy at the anticipation of it. The buzz I have from the white wine I gulped from a plastic cup at the office party adds to my jubilant mood.

"What are you doing for New Year's?" Chris asks.

"I'm going skiing in Park City with my friend Cathi and her family." He lifts his eyebrows, and I'm delighted to see that this news surprises him. I pat myself on the back for keeping this nugget of information to myself until this moment. It makes me mysterious. He doesn't know everything about me! Plus, it's Park City. I'm so cool, I ski where the celebrities ski. I don't tell him that besides the airfare, Mr. Render will pick up the tab for everything.

"I didn't know you skied," he says and turns to me, his head tilted to the side as he sidesteps a family walking four abreast, taking up the entire sidewalk. We both glare at them as we walk by.

"Sure do," I say. "I went to college in Vermont, remember?"

"Oh yeah," he says, and for a moment I'm worried that my withholding information was a mistake. I think, *I'd skip the trip if you told me you wanted to hang out for New Year's.* Instead I ask, "What are you doing?"

He gives me a vague answer, careful not to mention his girlfriend, Jill. Earlier in the week it was Chris's thirtieth birthday and his boss threw him a party at the office. It was a typical office party, awkward with cake in the conference room. A coworker started to mention something to the group about Chris's girlfriend Jill and Chris cut her off, speaking to her in German. It was a weird moment, not only because it's odd to find two people who can speak German in the same department, but also because he obviously didn't want that woman to say whatever she was about to say. Many years later I would witness Chris's parents do the same thing, but in Italian.

For tonight, I'm putting aside all the weird secrecy and vagueness. Tonight is my night. He's here with me, not his girlfriend. I go over the party details in my head. I hung strings of white lights around our living room. I found a special Christmas punch recipe with pomegranate juice, vodka, and Cointreau from the December issue of *Martha Stewart Living*. And I invited all the friends I have in the city. I even convinced my childhood friend Jennifer to come into the city from New Jersey. Jennifer is beautiful and smart, currently getting her doctorate. I will show Chris that I have interesting friends just like he does. That I'm fun and cool. I need him to realize what he's missing by not dating me. He'll wish he was with me instead of his girlfriend over the holiday break. And just in case the night heads the way I hope it will, I'm dressed for success. I have on a sparkly silver skirt, a top from the Gap, and underneath I have a matching lacy black bra and thong. My knee-high black leather Nine West boots complete the outfit.

The party goes well but it doesn't last long. It is one of those get-togethers where people stop by on their way to another party, and my apartment quickly clears out. Even Jennifer leaves early. I feel guilty that she traveled three hours, one and a half hours each way, to stay only an hour at the party. Normally I'd be upset that my party was lame, but I don't mind because now I'm alone with Chris, which was my ultimate goal anyway. And pretty much all the party guests knew that. Maybe that's why they got out of Dodge early. I hop up to sit on the kitchen counter, crossing my legs so the slit in my skirt reveals my stockinged thighs. I don't remember most of what I say. I've had a lot of punch. Chris is close to me, and I'm drunk enough to say, "I want to kiss you."

"I can't," he says, shaking his head, and he begins to turn away as if to leave, but then he turns back quickly and lays both hands on my cheeks. He kisses me long and hard. He then scoops me off the counter and carries me into my bedroom. We make out for a while, grasping at each other and rolling around on my bed. At some point my skirt and top come off and I'm only in my bra, thong, and boots. But each time I try to take it further, tugging at his belt, he pulls away.

"I can't," he keeps repeating as he kisses my neck. Finally he stops and says he must go. I get dressed and walk him down the three flights of stairs and outside to the street. As he lights a cigarette, he points to the neon sign that hangs over the St. Paul's House mission. "Sin Will Find You Out," it blares into the gray-black night sky of New York City. I've walked past that sign a gazillion times but never stopped to ponder it until Chris pointed it out. He asks me if I'm drunk, and I say "yes," surprised that he is even asking. *Of course I am; aren't you?*

"Why do you ask?"

"You keep repeating yourself," he says. My mouth pinches shut and my face flushes. The night is over. I want Chris to go now. We say a short goodbye at 51st and 8th and he heads to the subway entrance to take the Long Island Railroad train back to Huntington. Or maybe he's going to Port Authority to take the bus to Hoboken and see his girlfriend. At this point, I'm too drunk to care.

The next day I take the 11:06 a.m. NJ Transit train to Red Bank. I'm heading to my parents' house for the holiday break. On the train, I remember how Chris told me he knew I was drunk because I was repeating myself, and a wave of shame washes over me, mixing with the nausea of my hangover. I stare out the window at the graffiti-covered buildings whizzing by. I hate when my drunkenness is obvious to other people. I try so hard to drink like a normal person, have a good buzz but not do anything stupid or embarrassing. Well, there's nothing I can do about it now. I push my embarrassment and shame down to the pit of my gut.

At my parents' house I find and pack up my winter gear for the ski trip. I'm excited to go away after Christmas and grateful to Cathi's father for inviting me. This is the second Christmas after my sister Julia's death. I know from experience, too much experience, that it's going to suck. For days before and after Christmas there will be a sad tension in the air that no one will talk about. My mom will stay in the kitchen drinking her scotch while prepping meals. My dad will read in his armchair by the fire in the living room. No one will say anything about missing Julia and William. We will all pretend we don't feel the heavy sadness in the air.

I'm napping in my old bedroom, still nursing my hangover, when the phone rings. Not our main line but the kids' line, which is rarely used now that all the kids are out of the house. Well, Roseann and I are out of the house. Julia and William are dead. I answer it, thinking it will be Cathi going over last-minute details about our ski trip. But it's Chris. I don't remember giving him my number, but there's a lot I don't remember from last night. I mostly remember the shame of him saying, "You are repeating yourself."

I forget what we say to each other exactly. Something like "Listen, don't worry about it . . ." "I'm sorry I was so drunk . . ." "You're such a good friend, I don't want to screw up our friendship at the office . . ." The conversation ends and I feel lighter. That he called me means I didn't say or do anything too embarrassing. It will be less awkward when we return to the office after the holiday break. I'm not sure what will happen between us. Maybe we will be just friends. At this moment, I'm okay with that. I'm relieved my drinking didn't end our friendship. Work would be unbearable if we weren't friends. I get out of bed and notice that my hangover is gone. I decide to take a shower and see if Jennifer wants to go out tonight. It's ladies' night at the Globe.

Christmas goes as expected, depressing and painful. Two days later I practically run out the door to Newark Airport for my ski trip to Park City. On the first night of our trip, before going to sleep, I think about the kiss with Chris in my apartment after the party. And that night I have a stunningly realistic dream. Not only do I kiss Chris again in my dream, but we are together as girlfriend and boyfriend. I don't remember the details of the dream, just that I wake up surprised and happy. It feels so real. That day, while skiing, I revel in the beautiful scenery and the fresh mountain air. I feel the fog of grief lighten a bit.

The next night I go to sleep again thinking about Chris. And again I dream we are together. It is the one and only time in my life when I'm able to control the content of my dreams. For four nights in a row, while sleeping in the top bunk of a ski condo in Utah, I'm lost in a magical dream world in which I am with Chris and he does not have a girlfriend.

THE IN-BETWEEN

December 6, 2010, Part 3
Thirty-three days until sober

Chris calls back again and I keep repeating the same things: "I'm sorry . . ."

"It's over . . ."

"It only lasted four months . . ."

Chris wants details about Bob, about the night at the Marriott. But when I give him details, he erupts in a rage.

"Do you know what it is like to have to give a presentation when all I can think about is this!" I hear him slam his palm on the desk in his hotel room.

I barely respond. He tells me I'm being so cold. I listen to him cry as I stare out the window at the barren trees in the backyard and sip my vodka cranberry. I break the silence by saying I need to pick Ray up from school now, and I hang up on him.

I go to the bathroom to brush my teeth and wash my face. I don't want anyone at the preschool to smell the alcohol on my breath. If only I had known, by that point, the vodka was seeping out of my pores. I assess my condition in the bathroom mirror. *I'm barely buzzed*, I think, *I'm fine to drive.* (I was not.)

Julia has woken up from her nap and is watching *The Backyardigans* on the living room couch. She is clutching her yellow blankie. Her red curly hair is matted from sleep.

"Come on, Julia. It's time to get Ray." I try to keep my voice upbeat, so she doesn't realize her father and I are in a crisis.

When I open the sliding door of the minivan, empty juice boxes and discarded fruit snack wrappers fall out. I push everything back in and make a mental note to clean the car before Chris comes home from his business trip. If he saw this mess, he'd be pissed. Then I remember that he's already pissed. I have finally given him something legitimate to be angry with me about. You want to be mad at me? Forget spending too much money on groceries or the mess in the minivan. Here's a real reason, a torrid affair, all tied up in a bow for you. Now your anger is justified. I buckle Julia into the car seat and give her a kiss on the lips. I look at the mess and think, *fuck it.*

In the hallway of Ray's preschool, I see my friend JaneAnn talking to another mom. I'm glad she's distracted because I don't want to talk to her or to anyone today. Normally, we'd chitchat and make plans to go to the park. Like many mom friends, JaneAnn and I became close when Raymond and her son Owen became friends. A forced matchmaking at the park. As I got to know JaneAnn, I was relieved to discover how similar we are. Moms cut from the same diaper cloth. We both have two sons and a daughter, relatively the same ages. We both wear clothes from Target and rarely shower before pickup. We roll our eyes at the moms who show up in the pickup line all coiffed in their fancy boots with their designer handbags. We often bring the kids to McDonald's for lunch. *Gasp!* McDonald's! I'm so grateful to have a mom friend who I can be myself around.

But I can't hang out with anyone today, not even JaneAnn. We've had confessionals at the park, discussions about how sometimes we wish everyone would just go away, and how we've locked ourselves in the bathroom just to have a few minutes of peace. But I've never told her about Bob, and hopefully I've successfully hidden my drinking from her. Today there would be no lunch at McDonald's and no afternoon in the park. I need to get Ray and get home. I stand at the classroom doorway and lean up against the doorjamb in case I'm swaying.

"Ray did great today," says Mrs. M.

"Great!" I keep my reply short. I don't want my voice to slur. Ray flashes a wide grin and grabs his backpack.

"How did it go today?" I ask Ray in the car.

"So fun!" he says. "We dissected owl pellets! I found mice bones!"

"Gross," I reply, smiling at him in the rearview mirror. "You'll have to tell MeMa about that. She loves that stuff."

Back at the house, Julia and Ray have settled down on the couch to watch TV. The phone rings again. It's Chris. I repeat the same things I said earlier:

"It's over . . ."

"I'm sorry . . ."

"It only lasted four months . . ."

"I can't talk about this now; the kids are here." And I hang up on him again.

I hear the bus turn onto our street. Recently the bus driver discovered where we live, and since Michael is the only kid in our neighborhood, the driver drops him off at our front door instead of at the bus stop down the street. It's been a lifesaver on the days when Julia is napping. Michael steps off the bus, his red curls flopping around his head. *He needs a haircut*, I think. One more thing on my list.

"How was your day, Michael?" I ask as he pushes his way past me into the house.

"Fine," he replies, but in a dejected tone, and I immediately worry about whether he is making friends. I get the sense he is not fitting in with the other kids at school.

While Michael plops down on the couch next to Julia and Ray, I go into the kitchen to make myself another drink. I note that the bottle is almost empty. Taking my drink into my bedroom, I cautiously turn on the laptop, worried that if I turn it on Chris will jump on the computer and find more evidence. As quickly as I can, I attempt to delete any traces of any emails to or from Bob. Three days, I think. I have three days to get my shit in order. My body feels loose and the terror I felt previously has released its grip on my mind. Maybe things are not as bad as I thought.

Two years ago, back when we lived in Huntington, Long Island, Chris had what I learned was called an "emotional affair." He became intimate with a woman he commuted on the train with. How did I find out? He was being distant, and sensing that something was up, I went digging. Looking back on it now, it was obvious. He went around the house singing "Trapped" by Bruce Springsteen. When I combed through his side of the computer, I discovered an email from this woman. She expressed interest in Chris and wrote to him, "If and when you are ready, I'll be waiting." Instead of confronting him directly that day, I waited until Friday, when I knew they'd both be on the 5:15 p.m. LIRR train home from the city. Our Volkswagen Passat wagon was in the shop, so I happened to be in a rental car at the time. I could be incognito. I planned a stakeout at the train station. Unfortunately I had no childcare, so Michael and Ray were in car seats in the back. At the time I was a few weeks pregnant with Julia, Michael was three, and Ray was one and a half. I drove to the train station, parked near the platform, and waited for the train to arrive.

When the train pulled into the station, my pulse quickened and I started to sweat. Would he notice us right away in this rental car and wonder what the heck we were doing there? I had an excuse all ready to go: "Michael wanted to see the train and we thought it would be fun to greet you." But Chris didn't see us. I watched my husband and this other woman exit the train together, laughing and walking two by two with their arms touching. They walked together like that, attached like Velcro, through the parking lot to their cars. Even though it was what I had expected, seeing my husband so enamored with another woman was a punch in the gut. I thought about all the other acquaintances we knew who also commuted on this train, and how they all must know this was going on too. It was so obvious just looking at them! I felt like I might puke.

I tried to wait and see what else would happen; maybe they would kiss when they got to their cars. But Michael spotted his father and said, "Mommy, why aren't we saying 'hi' to Dad?" So I drove slowly through the train station parking lot to where Chris's car was parked. When Chris saw that I was there, the look of panic in his eyes revealed everything. If you were to look upon the scene from above, with me, Chris, and this other woman all standing next to our car doors, you'd see the triangle clear as day. I'll never forget the glance the woman gave Chris after she saw me. She raised her eyebrows and mouthed, "Is everything all right?" He dismissed her with a nod that seemed to say, "Just go."

Later, when the kids were all in bed, we hashed out the whole thing. Chris admitted to flirting with this woman, who was going through a divorce. He admitted that he enjoyed her attention. It fed his ego. He swore the relationship mostly occurred on the train, back and forth to the city, and that they never talked on the phone. I'm not sure why he lied about that, because it was such an easy thing to double-check. A week later I checked the phone records, and the call log revealed they talked on the phone every chance they could get.

Things were tough then. I was an emotional mess and, because I was pregnant, I couldn't wash away my feelings with alcohol. I spent hours scouring the computer for more evidence, to catch him in a lie. One time I spotted the woman's car in town, and I followed her back to her house. I hemmed and hawed about whether to leave the marriage or not. If I wanted to, this was my chance. But did I want to? I can't remember the title, but I bought a self-help book to help me work through whether or not I should stay. Having two young boys and a third child on the way complicated things. Was I ready to throw away this whole family because my husband flirted with someone else? Chris constantly emphasized that nothing physical ever happened and therefore it wasn't as much of a betrayal as I was making it out to be. We went to therapy and the therapist said to me, "I really don't understand why this is such a big deal to you." Eventually we stopped talking about it. We focused on our family and adjusting to having three kids. We would need a bigger car and a bigger house. We bought a minivan and then we bought the Cape and moved to New Jersey. I'm sure Chris hoped I'd be happier living closer to my family. He was tired of me distrusting him and just wanted me to be happy. We basically swept the whole ugly emotional affair under the rug.

Now I sip my vodka cranberry and scour the computer once again, but this time for evidence of my affair with Bob. I think: *Maybe we can just say "even steven" and move on.* Or maybe I will leave? Get a small apartment in a neighboring town. I picture a studio apartment with exposed brick walls, lots of light, and hanging plants. But can I support myself on my measly administrative assistant salary?

My Blackberry dings:

"I changed my flight. I'm coming home tomorrow. I'll be home before the kids get home from school so we can talk."

As I process the text, the air gets sucked out of the room. *No no no no no.* I don't want him to come home early. My head drops into my hands as I contemplate what to do next.

The alcoholic brain has an amazing way of keeping things hidden even from oneself. So, although I can't say I thought this consciously at the time, in retrospect I know the real reason I was so upset Chris was coming home early. It was not because I'd be forced to deal with the consequences of my affair sooner. Although that did suck. The main reason I was so upset Chris changed his flight was that I'd lose my uninterrupted drinking time. I was supposed to have three whole days of drinking the way I wanted to drink without having to hide it from Chris. Three days of drinking my vodka cranberry all day and all night. But his text meant that now I only had one day.

I'LL NEED A DRINK AND AN HOUR

Some month in 1999
Twelve years until sober

Chris and I are at the diner around the corner from the office, just north of Columbus Circle. We've been coming here for lunch at least once a week. Chris always wants to split a turkey sandwich with mayonnaise, Swiss cheese, and extra pepper. I always oblige his request even though I don't like Swiss cheese or might not be in the mood for a turkey sandwich. "Easygoing" is the vibe I strive to exude. I'm not sure what is going on with his girlfriend. He doesn't mention her, so I don't ask. But from what he's said, I gather she is high-maintenance. And I want him to know I'm not.

"Be careful," my cousin Peter, who is also my boss at the College Board, warned me when he learned Chris and I were spending time together.

"What do you mean?" I asked.

"He has a girlfriend. I don't want you to get hurt."

"I think it's over with her," I told Peter, although to be honest I'm not really sure. After the Christmas party, Chris and I have spent a few nights together. A couple of times we've gone out to dinner in the city and ended up back at my apartment.

Once, after a long, flirty phone conversation late at night, Chris convinced me to take a cab from the city out to his house in Long Island. I'm pretty sure the cab driver thought I was a hooker. But although we've consummated this relationship several times, it's still unclear what we are to each other. Are we still just friends? Friends with benefits? Are things officially over with his girlfriend? He doesn't tell me and I'm too afraid of the wrong answer to ask.

While waiting for the server to bring our sandwich to share, Chris tells me a story about his brother getting in trouble on a trip to Disney World. He is the youngest of seven and I love hearing about the antics of his older brothers and sisters. Every time he tells a story, I can feel myself drawn to this loud group of Italians.

On the surface, our families seem quite different—his are boisterous Italians living in Long Island, mine are reserved Irish/Germans living in New Jersey. And because of our ethnicity, Chris and I look very different. Chris is dark-skinned with a large nose and long dark eyelashes that frame his almond-shaped brown eyes. I'm light-skinned and freckled, with strawberry-blond hair. My eyelashes are so light you can barely see them, and my childhood friend used to make fun of me because my nostrils are so small.

But scratch the surface and you can see, we share fundamental similarities. Although from different parts of Europe, our grandparents are immigrants who settled in the outskirts of New York City hoping to have a better life than the ones they moved away from. We were both raised Roman Catholic, with a strong sense of family. We share stories of getting in trouble during weekly Mass. Both of our parents have been married thirty-plus years. His dad is a prominent pediatrician; my dad is a prominent federal judge. Our moms were early childhood educators, although Chris's mom didn't go back to work after raising her kids. My mother opened and ran a nursery school once her kids were school-aged.

But Chris is not the only one holding back vital information. I haven't yet told Chris about my family. In fact, he may have gotten misleading information. Depending on the situation, he may have overheard me answer the question, "How many siblings do you have?" differently. If I'm pretty sure I'm never going to see the questioner again, I might just say, "I have an older sister." Or if maybe I'll see them again, I might say, "I grew up the youngest of four." The "grew up" indicates that's how I grew up, though I'm no longer the youngest of four. It's complicated and I break into a sweat whenever the question arises.

Since we are on the subject of siblings, I'm forced to explain to Chris, "I had an older brother and sister who passed away." When I say it like this, as one sentence, it makes it sound like my brother and sister both died in one incident, a car wreck or a house fire. So I follow up with, "My brother died in a car accident, um, I guess eight years ago. My sister Julia died about a year ago."

Chris leans in and grabs my hand under the table. He looks at me expectantly, waiting for me to tell more of the story. I meet his eyes quickly and then turn away from his gaze.

"It's a long story," I say with a smile. "To tell it, I'll need a drink and an hour." I try to make light of the situation.

"Okay," he says. "Let's get a drink after work tonight." I nod and pull my hand away from his. I take a bite of my half of the turkey sandwich.

All day at work I'm an emotional mess. I know I need to tell Chris the story of my siblings, but once I do, I know how it will reflect on me. I'm damaged. My family is fucked up. I waver back and forth about canceling. I could just say I don't feel well.

But I'm so in love with Chris that I crave spending time with him. I would never turn him down.

Finally the moment arrives, and we meet outside our office building.

"Let's go downtown," Chris suggests. That seems like a good plan. I need to be in a different environment if I'm going to tell the full story. I need to be far away from work.

He flags down a cab and gives the driver the address. Having never spent much time in the lower part of New York City, I'm confused as to where we are. I need the grid of Midtown to orient myself. But Chris went to New York University; downtown is his old stomping grounds. He steers us to a hip Mexican restaurant, the Cactus Café, around the corner from the Bottom Line.

The waiter takes our drink order and we chitchat about work stuff until the margaritas arrive. I squeeze the lime and brush the salt off the rim into the milky yellow liquid, then take a deep sip of the tequila. I can feel my jaw unclench and my shoulders drop as the welcomed alcohol does the trick. I start with the easier story.

"My brother William died in a car accident when I was eighteen. He was twenty-one. He was drunk." I pause and take a sip of my drink. "No one else was injured in the crash," I rush to add, and think how much more horrible the story would be if it was more than just William veering off the Garden State Parkway into a tree. What if he had killed a family?

I continue, "My brother was always a fuckup. My parents sent him away to boarding school at first and then, when that didn't work, to rehab. He was sober for awhile, I guess. But then he started drinking again." I shrug. This story is straightforward. A wild one, my brother always seemed destined to crash and burn. Neil Young's lyric, "It is better to burn out than to fade away," always comes to mind when I think of William.

The waiter comes to take our order. I'm not really hungry so Chris and I opt to split a chicken burrito. The waiter glances at my drink, which I've made a significant dent in.

"Want another?"

"Sure. Thanks," I say. Chris's drink is still full. He takes a sip to catch up.

"My sister Julia . . ." I start and stop as tears have sprung to my eyes.

"About a year ago, my sister Julia overdosed on antidepressants." At this time in my life, I can't say "attempted suicide" or "intentionally overdosed." Every time I have had this conversation, the unfortunate person on the receiving end of these sentences must have been so confused. But in this moment, I look at Chris and he seems to understand what I'm saying. I don't need to clarify by saying, "She attempted suicide," and I breathe a sigh of relief.

"But she didn't die right away," I go on to explain. "She was in a coma at first . . ." my voice is getting softer. "Then she aspirated a chicken dinner and became septic. You see, she had ulcerative colitis when she was a teenager . . ."

This is when the story gets too complicated to tell. It's too difficult to explain what happened inside Julia's body after she purposefully overdosed on the antianxiety medicine. Too complicated to say that the stress of the overdose caused her previously reconstructed colon to burst, leaking shit throughout her body. She had a surgery to clean it out and then another surgery. How do I explain that we sat next to Julia's hospital bed for eight months, never really knowing if she'd get better? How, when the tracheostomy tube was finally removed, it became clear Julia's brain was damaged, either from the overdose or the aspiration? How I started to realize that for the rest of our lives we'd be taking care of an invalid, a shadow of my sister Julia? How, when her body gave out again and the surgeons said she needed another surgery to live but if we gave her another surgery she would die, I was relieved? I still to this day, twenty-eight years later, have trouble explaining the story of those eight months.

Chris has reached his hand over the table to grab mine. He holds it as I try to quickly wrap up the story. Can't we go back to telling funny stories about how we fainted in church and how angry our fathers got?

"Julia went from hospital to hospital for eight months. And eventually her body gave out and she died."

Chris squeezes my hand as I use the napkin to wipe my eyes. I need to stop talking about this. First, because it's too difficult. Also, because now Chris knows. Knows my family is a broken tragic mess with suicides and alcoholics. Who would want to date such a horrible mess?

The waiter delivers our burrito and an extra plate. "Do you want another drink?" he asks, seeing that my second margarita glass is empty.

"No thanks." I smile at the waiter. Of course I want one, but there is no way I can order a third drink when Chris hasn't finished his first. "Just a water, please."

After our meal, Chris asks if we can hit a clothing store so he can buy a shirt to wear to work tomorrow.

"Of course!" I say enthusiastically. So he is still coming back to my apartment tonight. He heard my tragic story, he knows my family is broken, and he is not running in the other direction. He's choosing to stay.

THERE'S ONE MORE THING . . .

December 7, 2010
Thirty-two days until sober

"I need some air," I say and walk out on the deck. I'm hoping to get away from Chris, but he follows me out there. He has cut his business trip short and arrived home this morning to deal with our broken marriage. I'm not sure what he told his boss. When he first walked in the door, after the kids had already left for school, I could see the hurt in his eyes and feel the pain oozing out of his pores. He was an open, festering wound and out of desperation we hugged and cried and ended up in bed together. We made love and clutched each other, hoping to smother the hurt, remove the oxygen and snuff out the burning flame of pain. But after we got out of bed, like a large gust of wind, reality came rushing back into the room, causing the pain to flare up. Now there is no longer any more tenderness, just accusations and anger.

Leaning up against the porch's rickety railing, I stare at the neighbor's yard, the bare oak trees silhouetted against the gray December sky. I didn't grab a coat, and I shiver a bit at the winter air. I realize that I'm wearing the same jeans and long-sleeved T-shirt I was wearing when Chris saw my email on the computer.

The last twenty-four hours have been a drunken blur. Last night I passed out in bed in my clothes, and I haven't changed. Chris lights a cigarette and begins pacing back and forth. I jump when he slams his palm down on the patio's wrought iron table. The table shakes and rattles.

We've just spent an hour dropping emotional bombs on each other. I would have done anything to be able to skip this discussion. *Just leave*, I plead in my head. But Chris wants to know the details and I'm resigned to the fact that this is happening, there is no way out of this full confession, so I give him details. How a flirtation with Bob at our college reunion led to Facebook messages. How things got out of hand. How we had one night together but now it is over.

"Is it over because he dumped you or because you want it to be over?" Chris asks.

I shrug. It's just over. I tell him what my therapist said: that I was unhappy, and the affair was a Band-Aid.

Chris has his own admissions. He is still keeping in touch with the train woman he had an emotional affair with back when we lived in Huntington, even though he had insisted time and time again that he never talked to her. And something happened with Robin, his coworker, and a friend of mine. Flirtations that never went anywhere. Nothing physical ever happened, he insists. In an angry huff, I claim his flirtations are worse. They've been happening for years and with several different women. One of the women is, or was, I guess, my friend. But it was never physical, he swears. My indiscretion with Bob is so much worse because I followed through with my flirtation.

We are on an emotional seesaw. Each revelation weighs the scale of the guilt up or down. But mine is worse because of that one night at the Marriott. He puts all his weight on the seesaw and keeps me suspended in the air, my legs dangling, and like a child I plead with him to let me down.

What happens next is something to this day I cannot explain. It is not something I planned or ever thought about doing. If this were a movie, the air would shift, a wind would blow through the yard. The light would flicker. Everything is about to change.

"There's one more thing," I say. I surprise myself. Even I don't know what I am about to say.

"Let's hear it," he says, taking a long drag on his cigarette. He glares at me with hurt and anger. I have to turn from his gaze. It's too intense.

"I drink," I say. "I drink vodka during the day. Not every day. But most days."

My heart drops into my stomach. *What have I done?* The words float in the air, and I wish desperately that I could grab them and shove them back into my mouth. Once this admission leaves my lips, I know what will happen next. I know because as a child I have been witness to this situation. My brother William admitted to having a drinking problem and my parents sent him to rehab. He attended Alcoholics Anonymous meetings, and my sisters and I were forced to attend an Al-Anon meeting. I know based on past experience that once I admit my drinking problem, I have to stop drinking. I do not want to stop drinking. Especially now with this shitstorm of a marriage we've just admitted to ruining. How am I going to survive this emotional roller-coaster ride without my precious vodka?

Chris smashes his cigarette into the ashtray.

"Well, that makes sense," he says. "At least that makes sense."

His demeanor has changed. His body relaxes and there is relief in his eyes.

"You must have known, Chris," I begin, immediately shifting

the focus off of me and onto him. Like a wild animal caught in a trap, I immediately start hissing and gnashing my teeth at him. I start listing the times when I was almost caught drinking.

"No," he stammers. "I had no idea."

I am done. I can't talk about this anymore. I can't rehash my affair over and over again. I don't want to hear about his flirtations with other women. And I certainly don't want to talk about my drinking with him. I walk away from Chris on the deck, walk out the front door, and sit on the stoop to wait for Michael's bus.

THE COURTYARD KISS

February 1999
Twelve years until sober

I'm cleaning off my desk, tossing old coffee cups and putting pencils into my drawer, killing time until it is acceptable to leave work, when an email from Chris pops up in my inbox. My cubicle sits right outside my boss's office, and she is in there typing emails and making phone calls. She will stay until late tonight inventing work so she doesn't have to go home to her empty Upper East Side apartment. I don't have anything or anyone to rush home to either, but I don't want to stick around the office any longer than I have to. I'm tired.

Today I tried to be strong and not flirt with Chris. I turned down his offer to go to lunch. And when we bumped into each other in the supply room and he asked me about my plans for the weekend, I was elusive, like he always is. I call this aloofness technique "Cold-Shoulder Liz."

I'm tired of this game he is playing. I like him and I know he likes me. But I guess he still has a girlfriend, even though he never mentions her. I want more than a casual hookup. I'm starting to feel used. That stupid phrase, "He won't buy the cow if he can get the milk for free," echoes in my head. And my roommate Kelly disapproves. We hang out at work all day, talking and having fun, but nothing ever goes anywhere and every night after work I go home alone. Work days when I'm with Chris I feel energized and lighthearted. But at night when I'm by myself in my apartment, I'm sluggish and depressed. Something needs to change.

"Want to get a drink?" Chris asks in the email. Cold-Shoulder Liz should say "no." I should move on like Kelly keeps telling me to do. But in this moment, I'm worn down. I don't want to go home to my empty apartment on a Friday night, drinking beers by myself and watching *Felicity* on the WB. It's pathetic. I hit reply and type out "Sure," then hesitate for a minute before hitting send. I don't have to reply. I could pretend I didn't see the email and bolt out of here. That would show him. Make it clear I'm not waiting around for him. But my resolve softens, and I click "send." He replies almost immediately, his enthusiasm coming through the email. "Great! Meet me in the lobby in ten minutes."

I head to the bathroom to freshen up before leaving. On my way, I peek over the row of cubicles and my heart skips a beat when I see Chris in his office, bustling around and packing up his stuff. Higher up on the work food chain than me, he gets an actual office with a window. I've logged many hours sitting next to his desk, chitchatting when we should have been working. In the bathroom, I sigh at my reflection. I have dark circles under my eyes and there is nothing to be done with my mop of curly, dirty-blond hair. *What does his girlfriend look like?* I wonder for the umpteenth time. I pull my hair back into a loose bun and brush on foundation powder to even out my skin tone. At least my outfit isn't so bad. It's casual Friday so I'm wearing my favorite pair of jeans and a sweater of Kelly's, which brings out the green in my eyes.

Back at my desk, I pack up my brown suede messenger bag and put on my down jacket. It has been cold, and the weather forecaster has predicted snow for tonight. I peek my head in

Mary Carroll's office to say goodbye and then head to the elevators. But then I see Chris headed there and I opt for the stairs instead. I need one more minute to clear my head before seeing him. As I plod down the stairwell, which is cold and smells like an ice-skating rink, my resolve strengthens and I repeat, "Cold-Shoulder Liz, Cold-Shoulder Liz," like a mantra. Enough is enough. Tonight I will tell him this whole charade has to stop. He can no longer have the cow, or is it the milk? Whatever. I want to be his girlfriend and if he doesn't want that then we have to stop hooking up.

I arrive in the lobby before the elevator. I'm standing by a bust of some historical figure, one of the many expensive pieces of art the College Board buys with its extra SAT money, when the elevator dings and the door opens and there is Chris. My hardened resolve melts when he looks at me and breaks into a wide smile. He has a way of focusing on me that makes everyone and everything else disappear. Although we are surrounded by coworkers, I feel like it's just us in our office lobby.

"Are we going to Rosa's?" I ask. That's our usual after-work spot: a Mexican restaurant with killer margaritas and homemade guacamole.

"Let's try someplace different," he says, and I follow him out the revolving doors and onto 9th Avenue.

"What about the bar at the Empire?" he asks.

I shrug and say sure, wondering if he is purposefully picking a spot where we won't run into anyone from work.

We walk the block uptown slowly so Chris can smoke a cigarette. I wait with him outside the Hotel Empire as he takes one last drag and then smashes out the butt in the gold receptacle by the door. He holds the door open for me and we enter the lobby. Something feels weird. Sleazy, as if we were sneaking around, having an affair.

We take our seats at the bar, which is upstairs and has a good view of Lincoln Center. Behind Avery Fisher Hall, you can see the white tent set up for the Big Apple Circus.

"My friend Julie is going to the circus tonight," Chris says. *Great*, I think, *more female friends*. Does he keep her on the side like he does with me? Chris orders his usual, a Maker's Mark. Instead of a beer, I get a vodka gimlet. I've recently discovered this drink and love its immediate effect. I'd have to drink three beers to feel like I do after just one gimlet. Plus, it seems more sophisticated, and tonight that's the vibe I want to give off. I'm not that bumbling girl from suburbia who mistakenly plugged her computer into Chris's monitor at the conference booth back in April. Tonight I'm a sophisticated working woman who doesn't have time to waste.

Chris tries to talk about people we work with, the ridiculousness of the College Board, and how crazy it was that the president gave the whole company Blockbuster gift cards to rent the movie *October Sky*, but I refuse to join in. I don't want to talk about this superficial stuff anymore. I want to talk about us. I want to know what's going on.

I don't remember if I say anything or if Chris reads my mind based on my lack of responses to his conversation starters, but at some point he says, "Let's go for a walk." He has half a glass left of bourbon, but my gimlet is gone. I'd love to order another one, but I can tell I'm finally going to get an explanation about what is going on between us, so I say okay. Chris pays the bill and I gather up my stuff.

We walk in silence, crossing Broadway, heading towards Central Park. A light snow begins to fall. The cold gives the night air a crisp and clean feeling, even with the smoke billowing from the taxicabs. Tomorrow, when the temperature warms and the accumulated snow turns to dirty slush, the city will once again feel like a place for the downtrodden. But tonight, New York feels fresh and full of possibilities.

We pass by Lincoln Plaza Cinema, and I note *Rushmore* is playing. Chris loves Wes Anderson movies and we've been talking about skipping out of work to see this one. But he hasn't mentioned it in a while, so that probably means he saw the movie with his girlfriend. We are still heading towards the park when we both notice a courtyard between buildings off of 63rd and instinctively walk into the spot. Several benches line the courtyard, but they are empty. We are alone. We both stop in the center and turn to stare at each other. I refuse to say anything. Chris needs to speak first, and he knows it.

Minutes go by and I'm ready to give up. I start to turn away, to head home, when he grabs my hands, warming them in his. He looks at me intensely with his dark almond eyes. He knows I'm close to giving up on him, and his eyes plead *don't.*

"I think I'm falling in love with you," Chris says.

I don't know how to respond to this. He knows how I feel. I don't need to tell him that the minute he gives me the go-ahead, I am his. But does he know how much this waiting is torturing me?

"You're breaking my heart," I respond. His face crumbles and we lean into each other. Still holding hands, we touch foreheads, as if we could explain our feelings through our skin, through osmosis. Then we kiss. Not a sloppy, drunken, post-holiday-party kiss, but a tender, caring, we-need-each-other kiss. My legs weaken and I lean into him. I know that from that moment on, he is mine. It doesn't happen as fast as I would like. Going forward there is some overlap between our relationship and the one with his girlfriend Jill. But in the end, he and I will be together. I'm certain of that as we kiss in the secluded courtyard and snow gently falls in New York City.

THERAPY AND MORE THERAPY

December 7–8, 2010
One month until sober

After my admission on the deck, Chris and I manage to get through the rest of the day by focusing on the normal day-to-day duties of parents. We get the kids from school, feed them dinner, help them with homework. We don't talk or make eye contact. Due to the renovation our house is now bigger, with its dormers and an extra bathroom, but it feels ten times smaller. I'm suffocating. I want Chris to go away, just leave me be, but since he left the conference early, he has the rest of the week off from work. He is on an emergency leave. Again I wonder what he told his boss. My face flushes hot with shame.

The next morning, after we get the boys off to school, I'm at a loss for what to do with Chris in the house. I hear him slamming things around in the bedroom and I think we will kill each other if we don't take some sort of action. Luckily Julia is around, which makes us behave better. Neither of us wants to fight in front of the kids, although it still happens. It's Wednesday and I happen to have a therapist appointment that afternoon, so I suggest Chris come with me. We will drop Julia off at my mom's on our way.

I started seeing Dr. Michelle Rabinowitz soon after the affair ended. I was emotionally wrung out, unable to function as a wife and a mother. And although I wouldn't have been able to tell you at that time, part of me knew my drinking was out of control. At this point I was drinking every day. I had even shown up drunk to some of my therapy appointments.

When Chris and I sit down in the therapist's waiting room, the receptionist takes one look at us together and jumps out of her chair and runs into the back room. Something is wrong. We've made a mistake by both coming. As we wait in the plush chairs, I am numb, but I can feel the anger pulsating from Chris. After a few minutes, we get ushered into Michelle's office. We get settled in our seats and she raises her arms in a shrug, asking silently: *What is going on here?*

Chris does all the talking. He found out about the affair. And by the way, Liz admitted she has a drinking problem. If the latter news shocks Michelle, she hides it well. As Chris talks, I can feel Michelle's annoyance grow. We shouldn't have both come. Chris is mad at me and now my therapist is too. Everyone agrees I'm a worthless piece of shit.

When Chris is done talking, Michelle responds. First of all, she is not a marriage therapist. She is my therapist, and Chris should not have come to the appointment. He should find his own therapist. She can provide some recommendations. Also, she doesn't handle recovery issues. She will continue to see me, if I'd like, but she recommends that I also see an alcoholism counselor.

At some point, Chris complains to Michelle that I won't talk to him, that I shut down and shut him out. I'm getting ready to balk at this when Michelle agrees with him.

"Yes, Liz puts up walls with me too," she says to Chris. I sit back in my seat. *What is she talking about?* I'm aghast! Why would I put up walls with my own therapist? I certainly don't feel like I am. Michelle tells Chris he should consider Al-Anon, a fellowship that offers a program of recovery for the families of alcoholics. I nod when she says this.

"I went to Al-Anon when I was a teen, for my brother." They both stare at me like I have two heads. I realize maybe I shouldn't speak. No one wants to hear what the fuckup has to say. In the car on the way home, I slump down in the passenger seat with the weight of everyone's disappointment.

"I'll call the alcoholism counselor when we get home." Chris doesn't respond. I'm not sure how he thought this appointment would go but it wasn't to his liking. Silence settles like poured concrete in between me and Chris.

December 15, 2010
Twenty-four days until sober

A week later, I return to Michelle's office by myself for my normal weekly appointment. The receptionist nods at me. *You didn't bring your husband, good job,* her nod seems to say. *Great,* I think, *just what I need, condescension from my therapist's receptionist.*

I tell Michelle about the fights Chris and I are having. I tell her how I repeat over and over again: "It only lasted four months. It was only one night." And by the way, what Chris did was worse. He had multiple emotional affairs. She listens to me rant but doesn't agree with me. I will learn later a phrase that applies here: "She doesn't cosign my bullshit." I tell her how Chris wants details, how I try to avoid telling him, but he presses, and I give in.

"Wow," Michelle says, shocked at what I've revealed to Chris. "You really went for the jugular there. You said the exact thing that would hurt Chris the most."

"I know," I say, shifting in my leather chair. I look down and straighten the leg of my jeans. "I know," I repeat. I can feel her gaze on me.

I should feel like shit. I've done such bad things. I've said hurtful things. I've been drunk on and off for ten years and kept it a secret. And then I really fucked up. I mean a colossal, martial fuckup. And yet I still feel justified. Righteous even. He's done horrible things too: my constant mantra. It's like that scene from *The Breakfast Club* when Judd Nelson as John Bender says, "What about you, Dad? What about you?" I keep saying, "What about you, Chris? What about you?"

Michelle doesn't say much. She lets me absorb the situation I've put myself in. Shows me the pit that I've purposely fallen into. More like jumped into, knowing there was no ladder to get me out.

"Let's talk about your recovery plan," she says, shifting the conversation away from the arguments Chris and I are having. I look around the room and stare at the picture of her twin kids.

"I had one appointment with that woman you recommended, MaryAnne . . ." I say to Michelle. "Although, I don't know . . ." I trail off.

I didn't connect with MaryAnne. Her office was a cold annex, a sunroom off her house. I had to drag Julia to the appointment, which was awkward. Even though she is only two years old, I still don't want to say anything too damaging in front of my daughter. Also, MaryAnne kept focusing on my mother and her drinking. She asked if my mother was losing her tolerance to alcohol because that was one of the symptoms of alcoholism. I found myself defending my mother to this stranger, who obviously has mother-daughter issues of her own.

"MaryAnne told me to go to an AA meeting, so I'm going tomorrow night. An all-women's meeting."

Michelle brightens at this news and wraps up our conversation. I leave feeling dejected. I want someone to solve my problem. I want to hand this big pile of shit to Michelle and say, "Fix it."

On the drive home, I pass by a house with a deflated inflatable Santa decoration on the front lawn. He is slumped over himself and I think, *Rough night, Santa?* I review my sessions with Michelle. Although she says she is not a recovery therapist, I don't want to stop seeing her. She is the first therapist I have had who knows my whole story. My family's tragedies, my affair, and now, that I am an alcoholic.

The first therapist I saw was Dr. Varga. When I was fifteen and a high school sophomore, I revealed to my mother how depressed I was. There was a boy I liked. He didn't like me back. Also, I was binging and purging. I couldn't stop. Late at night, I would stuff down pecan sandies or peanut butter and crackers. Then I'd tickle the back of my throat with my index finger and force myself to throw it all up. Off I went to the family psychologist, the same doctor my older sister Julia and my father saw for their anxiety problems. He prescribed antidepressants for me, and I did start to feel better. But I stopped taking them because I wanted to drink at an upcoming Grateful Dead concert and the doctor had warned me, "You can't drink and be on these antidepressants."

"I feel much better," I declared to my mom, and I weaned myself off the drugs. She stopped buying pecan sandies and we didn't talk about it anymore.

Then there was the doctor on the Upper West Side I saw right around the time Chris and I started dating. I don't remember her name, but I can remember the walks I took from my office at Lincoln Center up Columbus Avenue once a week. She was a dream analyzer, and we both got excited when I told her I had a dream in which I was trying to walk up Columbus

Avenue to get to her office but there was all this debris in the way, dilapidated buildings and broken construction materials. I would try to climb over the refuse, but I couldn't reach her office. I laughed at how easy it was to analyze that dream.

That therapist probably could have helped me if I had admitted how much I was drinking at the time. How I would wait until I had a night by myself in the Hell's Kitchen apartment I shared with Kelly. I'd buy myself a six-pack of Sierra Nevada beer or Mike's Hard Lemonade and drink it while listening to sad songs on my Sony Walkman. The lyrics from "This Woman's Work" by Kate Bush would inevitably cause me to break down, curl into a fetal position, and bawl.

But just like the other therapist I had seen, I avoided telling this doctor about my drinking.

When Chris and I got engaged, I stopped seeing that therapist. Actually, I ghosted her before "ghosting" was a term people used. I skipped the last appointment, stopped taking her calls, and didn't pay for the session I missed.

One day, soon after September 11th, I forgot to screen my calls, and I picked up the phone. It was my therapist. She was reaching out to all her former patients to see if they were still alive. Morbid but true. And if they were, how were they handling the aftereffects of the September 11th terrorist attacks? She was really so kind. I told her about my engagement and said things were much better now. I sent her a check in the mail. And at that time, it felt like that was a closed book on my mental health. I was engaged. Marriage was going to be what fixed me. That was what my problem was. I needed a loving partner, and everything would be fine.

Obviously, that turned out not to be true.

OUR HONEYMOON

October 2001
Ten years until sober

Chris and I are in Martha's Vineyard on our honeymoon. We picked a vacation spot within driving distance of our Long Island home because neither of us wanted to get on an airplane a month after the September 11th terrorist attacks.

I'm sitting on a chaise lounge poolside, flipping through the latest issue of *Real Simple*, waiting for Chris to finish swimming laps. The October sky is gray, and the air is warm and thick with moisture, like it might rain soon. Occasionally, a gust of wind sends brown and yellow leaves spiraling down from above. I put the magazine down and get the pool skimmer. Walking around the pool, I skim out the dead leaves, as Chris continues to do laps. Slow and steady, his arms rotate like a windmill while his black bathing cap cuts a path through the heated pool.

"It's warm," Chris says as he catches his breath at the end of the pool. "Come on in."

"Maybe later," I respond, even though I know there is no chance I'm going in. I barely swim during the hottest days of August. I'm not going in the pool in October no matter how warm he says it is.

Chris planned the entire honeymoon, from the location to the inn reservations. He saw it as his duty as the groom. So far, I'm happy with his choices. Taking the ferry across to Martha's Vineyard was cool. Because it's the offseason, the island is practically deserted, and it feels like we are the only two people in the world—a welcome change after the chaos of the wedding and the stress of dealing with our families. The inn he booked is perfect. We have a whole cabin with a sitting room and a deck. Everything is white—the walls, the furniture, the bedding—giving the cabin a clean, crisp feel. Behind our cabin is a wood with trails, and Chris has promised we will walk them soon. He also wants to go for a bike ride into town. I'm trying to be a good sport. I want to be the type of wife who is game for fun adventures, but I'm still recovering from a horrible cold I got on the day of the wedding.

The one downside to the inn is that it's located in a "dry" section of Martha's Vineyard. We found this out the previous night at dinner, when I tried to order a drink at the inn's restaurant. The waiter explained that it was BYOB, and that I needed to buy alcohol from another town on the island and bring it to dinner. It's inconvenient, but not the end of the world, I guess. Chris doesn't care because he doesn't even like to drink. He has his weed, which he has been smoking periodically throughout the day. But I was disappointed last night. I wanted the first night of our honeymoon to be a celebration, a party. Instead, it was kind of boring. For tonight's dinner, I suggested to Chris that we go to a different town.

Chris is finished swimming and we go back to our cabin so he can shower. I move to the chaise lounge on our deck, bringing my magazine and the box of tissues. When he's dressed, he goes to the inn's main office to find out where we can rent bikes for this afternoon's excursion. While he is gone we get a delivery, a large cellophane-wrapped gift basket from our coworkers. It includes a bottle of champagne, a bottle of wine, cheese and crackers, and fruit. I show it to Chris when he returns but he barely acknowledges it. He's eager to plan our bike ride and unfolds a map of Martha's Vineyard on the coffee table to plot our route.

"It's seven miles to the state forest. Then, we can cut through here and head up to Oak Bluffs." I'm starting to think I'd prefer to hang out in our cabin with the gift basket, specifically the bottle of champagne. And I think about suggesting it, but I see how excited he is about the bike ride. We can pop the champagne later.

We ride our bikes on a paved path through the pine shrubs and sandy hills of Martha's Vineyard. We come to a town and are lucky to find a pub open for lunch. Most of the island is closed for the season. We both order French onion soup and a beer. I finish my beer but not my soup. Chris finishes the soup but not his beer. We rode fifteen miles to get to this town and now we have to turn around and ride fifteen miles back to the inn. I'm full and tired from the soup and beer. When I get back on the bike, my legs revolt. They don't want to pedal. Chris gets way ahead of me on the path and I'm struggling to keep up. I force my legs to push another turn of the pedal. Tears stream down my face from the pain in my legs.

"Wait up!" I yell to Chris as I hop off the bike and walk it up the small hill. I curse him in my head. He knew I was sick; why did he plan such a long bike ride? Why couldn't we just sit at the cabin and drink and have sex like normal honeymooners? With each hard push of the pedals, my anger towards Chris grows. When we finally get back to the cabin, Chris goes to return the bikes and I collapse on the fluffy white comforter.

"Sorry it was such a long bike ride," Chris says when he returns, lying next to me on the bed. We finally do what normal honeymooners do: have sex and nap.

After resting for the remainder of the afternoon, I finally feel recuperated enough to get up and get ready for dinner. Before I get in the shower, I open the bottle of champagne and find plastic cups. I offer a glass to Chris, who declines. He is strumming on his Backpacker, a mini guitar he takes on trips, playing Bob Dylan's "The Man in Me," one of the two songs he played at our wedding. I try to read his face to see if he's annoyed I opened the bottle, but I can't tell.

I have one more plastic cup of champagne as we dress for dinner. At dinner, I order a beer and Chris gets water. I finish my drink halfway through the fish entrée and I want to order another one, but I feel awkward. Chris isn't drinking. I can't just drink on my own; that would be weird.

Chris suggests coffee and dessert. I can feel the buzz of the champagne and the beer wearing off and I'm getting antsy. Instead of coffee and dessert, I'd rather go sit at the bar and order more drinks, but I know that is not what Chris wants to do. He doesn't drink. Not the way I drink. He drinks for show. Meaning he will order a beer or a bourbon and sip from it because it's the social norm, but he rarely finishes it. I knew this when I married him, but it never occurred to me that it would be a problem. Usually we are hanging out with his friends, Ben, Mark, and Adam, who all like to drink as much as me. Or, if we did go out on a date just the two of us, I could have one or two drinks knowing that the next night I'd be alone and could have as many drinks as I wanted. Now, at this dinner, as my buzz wears off, this consequence of marrying Chris becomes clear. He doesn't drink the way I drink. When we are together like this, I cannot drink the way I want for fear of him noticing that I drink differently. That I drink too much. And now we are together forever. These are not conscious thoughts and feelings, but somewhere in my subconscious they are developing, and

I'm starting to feel squirmy inside. How is this going to work? When we return from this trip, we will live together. I will no longer live at my parents' condo, where I can steal nightly glasses of my mother's scotch. Now I'll be with Chris every night in our tiny cottage on the bay. I see the future ahead of me. My chest tightens and I feel trapped.

Our week in Martha's Vineyard is over. It's time to pack up and leave our cabin. My cold is almost gone, and I feel ready to get back to work. As we pack up our bags, Chris tells me the guys want to jam tonight at the studio when we get back to Long Island.

"Do you want to come?" he asks.

"No, you go. I'll stay home and write thank-you cards," I say as I load the gift basket with the unopened bottle of wine into the car.

NOWHERE TO GO

Mid-December 2010
A few weeks until sober

I'm awakened in the middle of the night by Chris slamming his fist on the bed. Not on me, which I'm sure he wants to, but right next to me. My whole body lifts with the force of his pounding on the mattress, like he's trying to ding the bell in a carnival game with his fists and my body is the puck. I jump to my feet, away from his wrath.

"You had Cathi lie for you." Even in the dark, I can see the spit flying out of his mouth and his finger jabbing at me, punctuating his point.

I've never seen him this angry before. I know there is no talking my way out of this moment. I must get away. For my safety. For both of us. I grab my purse and double-check that the car key is in there. Thank God my Converse sneakers are right by the front door. I slide them on my feet as a run out of the house and into the cold December air.

My usual response when Chris points out that I lied is to say, "Yeah, it was an affair and lying is part of the affair." He focuses on the duplicity, which seems secondary to me. I had an affair; of course I lied. But to him the lying is extra. I don't know how he thinks I could have an affair without lying. It's baffling to me.

I was worried he was going to figure out this part of the betrayal. That, in order to plan a weekend escape with Bob, I created a fake girls' weekend away and I employed my best childhood friend, Cathi, to help me with the deceit. She sent an email to me detailing the fake trip, which I forwarded to Chris.

"What do you think about me going to Boston with Cathi and her friends?" I wrote to Chris. Now Chris feels double-crossed and embarrassed. He had been played for a fool. More than that, Cathi was his friend too. He has a right to be pissed.

I steady my shaky hands by gripping the steering wheel. At the intersection, I pause. Where do I go? I can't go to my parents' condo at this hour; it's too late. Same with my sister's. I haven't told Roseann about my troubles, and I'm not about to at one in the morning. Once again I am helpless and trapped. Even if I want to leave this marriage, I don't know how I can. I have no money of my own. I can't afford rent on an apartment. A car pulls up behind me and I must move. Do I go left or right? I need to make a decision. I realize I don't need to figure out my entire life right at this moment. I only need to find a safe place to sleep tonight. A hotel is my only choice. Chris might be upset at the extra expense, but I have no other options. Hopefully Chris doesn't cancel our credit cards. I flip on my right blinker and drive the mile and a half to the Courtyard Marriott.

"Are you here visiting relatives for the holidays?" the front desk receptionist asks. *Is she kidding me?* I have tears and snot running down my face, my eyes are swollen from crying, and I'm in my pajamas, for pity's sake; does it look like I'm visiting relatives? I shake my head "no" and grab the room key.

I push open the door and survey the room. There is no minibar. I can't tell if I'm happy or sad about that. Then I remember that next to the front desk is a snack bar with a refrigerator. And in the refrigerator is a chilled, mini bottle of white wine. Did I notice that when I checked in? I guess so. I sit on the edge of the bed and contemplate going back to the front desk. What would the front desk lady think of me if I bought one or maybe even three mini wine bottles at one in the morning, with tears running down my face?

You don't know her, the devil on one of my shoulders says. *Who cares what she thinks?*

How are you going to pay for it? the angel on the other shoulder says. *You are going to spend money not only on this hotel room but also on wine? Think about how mad Chris will be then.*

In the end, the angel wins. I take off my shoes, pull back the covers, and climb into the bed. I turn on the TV and flip around until I find *Law & Order* and zone out to the familiar and soothing *chung chung* sound.

I allow myself to think about Bob for a minute. I still wish he hadn't ended things the way he did. I feel like I deserve some sort of closure. But what is clear now is that I have no interest in pursuing that relationship ever again. For the hundredth time, I fantasize about a huge eraser that could scrub away that section of my past—from the college reunion until the day Chris found the email.

Early the next morning, my Blackberry chimes. Chris texts: "Where are you?"

"At the Courtyard Marriott," I text back.

"I'm sorry about last night. I will leave for work when you come home."

He is calling a truce because he knows we have to get back to the business of raising this family. He will go to work, I'll get the kids' lunches packed and get them off to school. Then I'll go to work. We will deal with this festering wound later.

"Okay," I text back.

There is a new front desk person this morning, a dude. I look down and hurry past him. Out in the parking lot, I note a heaviness in the air that means snow is on the way.

LONG-TERM PARKING

December 2002
Nine years until sober

The airport shuttle bus lets us off in Lot D of JFK airport's long-term parking. Chris hoists his garment bag onto his shoulder and starts walking with purpose through the parked cars. He either remembers where the car is parked or is pretending to remember. I follow ten steps behind, wheeling my suitcase, hoping he doesn't know. The satisfaction I would get from his being wrong would outweigh the hassle of having to find the car.

Currently we are giving each other the silent treatment. We didn't say one word to each other the entire flight home from San Francisco. We were in Pebble Beach, CA, to attend my company's holiday party, a party I don't entirely remember. The only evidence that I had fun is the pounding headache behind my right eye. I didn't dare order a drink on the airplane when the flight attendant offered, but if I had, I would feel better now. Hair of the dog. The crisp December air helps to clear my groggy head, even with the car fumes coming off the traffic-choked Van Wyck Expressway.

Chris finds his car easily. Now that we are married, I guess technically it's our car. But it doesn't feel that way, even after a year of marriage. When will things feel like "ours" instead of just his? I moved to his town, live in his house, eat at his table, sleep in his bed. I am an intruder in his life. "Our" car is an old brown Mercedes sedan that maybe was once nice but is well past its glory days. Eventually we will get a new car, but this one suits us for now since we mostly use it to drive back and forth to the train station, commuting to New York City on the Long Island Railroad.

Chris still works as a program director at the College Board. I am five months into a new job as an associate producer for a travel website. I was miserable at my old job and eager to find something else, but this new job isn't turning out so great either. It has a writing component, which I like. I draft fun, bubbly pieces encouraging subscribers to take weekend getaways. But it also has a sales component. Having no prior sales experience, I struggle to understand the subtleties of sales and often fail, to the dismay of my supervisor.

Adding to my stress is that this new job has caused a shift in my relationship with Chris. I now work longer hours than he does, and we often don't catch the same train home. When we both worked at the same company, we would commute together on the train in the morning, we were in meetings with each other, we'd have lunch together, and then we'd commute home together at night. Personally, I welcomed the separation my new job introduced. I can't say the same for Chris.

Chris opens the trunk of the car and carefully lays his garment bag inside, then waits for me to catch up. He refuses to look at me as he grabs my small suitcase out of my hand and puts it in the trunk. He slams down the trunk lid and gets behind the wheel. Reluctantly, I open the passenger side door and slump down on the brown, cracked leather seats with a sense of dread. If I had any other way home at this moment, I would take it. I don't want to have the conversation we are about to have.

As we navigate our way through the parking lot to the exit, I try once again to remember what happened the night before that would have gotten Chris so angry. Was it just because I was a drunken mess in general, or did I do something horrible?

When the owners of the travel company, two German brothers, announced at a staff meeting the plan for our holiday party, we all whooped with excitement. A trip to California to stay at a four-star oceanfront resort. Wow! And we each could bring a guest. But the reality was that the trip was a huge hassle. We didn't get a day off from work to travel, so we had to leave Friday after work and return on Sunday. It was a long flight for such a short trip.

I replay the events of the previous night's holiday party in my head. I was so uncomfortable at the formal dinner. My hair was frizzy because a storm had caused the power to go out as I was getting dressed and I was unable to blow-dry my hair. My dress was frumpy. I felt old and out of place among my coworkers, who are younger and single. During the formal dinner, the two German owners introduced each employee with an interesting story and a word of praise. I squirmed in my seat when they got to me. All they said was: "Liz had to manage a new account on her first day." No praise, just a fact. I smiled and kept sipping my wine.

The only fun part of the night was the after-party in my supervisor's hotel suite. I had switched from wine to vodka tonics. That's when things start to get fuzzy. Chris kept saying, "It's time to go," but I wanted to stay because the party, the real party, was just starting. Someone suggested we do shots. I may have been flirting with my supervisor when Chris finally dragged me out of the party. I don't remember.

The next morning I was too hungover to care why Chris wasn't speaking to me. At least I had enough sense to set the alarm to wake up for the limo back to the airport. I rolled out of bed and put my frizzy hair in a ponytail. I had fifteen minutes to pack up my stuff, but I kept bolting to the bathroom to throw up. Chris packed up his own bag but refused to help me. It took every ounce of energy I had to stuff myself into the limo with my coworkers to get to the airport on time for our return flight.

On the plane I tried to talk to Chris, who just glared at me with that look. The one that says, *I am so disappointed in you.* Instead of guilt, I surged with anger. My anger was still pulsating as we got off the plane and walked to long-term parking to get the car.

After we pay the parking fee, I can no longer handle the silent treatment.

"I am so sorry. I didn't mean to drink so much," I say, my voice shaking as the tears begin. As I apologize, I realize that I'm about to admit to Chris, my husband for over a year, that I always drink too much. That once I start drinking, I can't stop until I pass out. That sometimes, on the nights when he is not around, I drink by myself. I drink a six-pack of beer or whatever alcohol is around until I pass out. I'm about to admit to Chris that I have a drinking problem. A problem I've struggled with since I was seventeen years old. This makes me sob harder.

"It's okay." Chris grabs my hand and brings it to his lips. "Why are you getting so upset? You had too much to drink but it's really not that big of a deal. I was just mad because you passed out when we got back to the room, and we didn't have sex. You know how much I love hotel sex." Now that I've apologized, Chris is no longer angry. Now that I've proven to him that it is all my fault, he wants me to stop blubbering.

As he is talking, it dawns on me. He is not going to tell me I cannot drink. He doesn't know. He doesn't realize I have a drinking problem. He thinks I just had one too many at the company's holiday party. It's a cliché, even. I'm off the hook.

"Okay," I say, wiping my eyes with the sleeves of my sweatshirt. "Okay, I'm sorry," I say as I sit up in the seat. I reel in whatever words were about to come out of my mouth.

Back at home, in our small house on the shores of Huntington Bay, we make love in our bed. Not hotel sex, which is wilder, but still, we had fun for a Sunday night. We never again talk about how I had too much to drink at the company holiday party. In fact, we never talk about my drinking again. From that point on, I learn to keep it in check in social situations. I only allow myself to get fall-down, pass-out drunk when I am by myself. Because I don't want anyone, especially Chris, to tell me I have to stop drinking.

PATHS THROUGH A BLIZZARD

December 26, 2010
Thirteen days until sober

Due to blizzard conditions, New Jersey declares a state of emergency on Sunday, December 26, 2010. Like some crazy cosmic joke, after spending a torturous Christmas together, Chris and I are now stuck in the house. All roads and modes of transportation are shut down. We are trapped.

The sun set about an hour ago, but the outdoor spotlights light up most of our backyard. Chris is outside, maintaining his paths. As soon as there was enough accumulation, Chris went outside to shovel. First he shoveled the sidewalks and driveway and cleared off the cars, then he started making paths through the yard. He spent hours bent over, heaving snow up into the air, making a maze of paths in the three-foot-high snow. It does makes it easier for the kids to play outside, especially for Julia, whose short legs can't navigate the deep drifts. But why so many paths? They criss-cross from the shed to the play fort, around the oak tree to the back deck. They don't lead anywhere. There's no escape.

I'm aware that I should feel something as I look out at Chris. I should feel guilt over my digressions, anger over his, sadness, or even relief. But I feel nothing. It's all blank. Chris would say I'm cold, but that's not quite right. It's not that my feelings are cruel. I don't have feelings. I have nothing, an absence of any feelings, like a black hole. I'm vacant.

It's easier for both of us when Chris stays outside. When he's inside, the house is cramped and stifling. Ironic, because the renovation is finished. After months of dealing with carpenters, electricians, and plumbers, the house is finally whole and quiet. Later, after I've been sober for a while and my feelings return, I will cringe when I think of the times I was drunk around Christian the contractor. Did he ever notice there was a slur in my speech, a stumble in my step during the day? He could have called Child Services. He probably should have. In the future, my body will flush with embarrassment when I realize that Christian must have been present for some of the screaming and crying in the days after Chris discovered the note on the computer. But all those feelings don't come until later.

The kids were so happy to finally move from their temporary, makeshift bedroom in the office to their expanded rooms upstairs, with new carpet and fresh paint: Disney's "Blushing Piglet Pink" for Julia and "Atta Boy Blue" for the boys. The bathroom is gorgeous, with white and black subway tile and double sinks. It's probably the best room in the house. The renovations are complete just as our life collapses. Now the house looks nice but neither Chris nor I want to be in it. Our quaint Cape is now dirty with secrets and lies. And then, the three feet of snow fell, keeping us all trapped together inside with the tension.

Earlier today I had told Chris I couldn't talk about it anymore, the discussions and accusations that go around and around and never get resolved. I was done. He hates that I can shut down like that and demands that I give him more time.

He even followed me into the kids' bathroom, where I went to take a bath in the new bathtub. "Don't you care? We are going to lose all this," he yelled, gesturing at the air. I'm not sure what he is referring to. The house? The marriage? I remained silent but in my head I thought, *I don't care.* I'm not sure I want any of this. I don't know how I ended up here.

VODKA AGAIN

April 13, 2008
Three years until sober

I steer my minivan next to the sidewalk that leads to the front door of my parents' condo, trying to get as close as possible without scraping the black pines that line the driveway. I put the car in park and push the button that automatically opens the van's passenger door.

"Thanks again, Mom and Dad. It was a great show." I try to sound grateful but the words come out flat and tired.

"Well, thanks for driving," my mother replies. She slowly turns toward the open door, grabbing onto the armrest and the front seat with her arthritic hands to position herself so that she can step out. Minivans are great for loading and unloading kids, but the captain seats and the high floor make it difficult for my sixty-nine-year-old mom to get in and out. She swings one leg around, gathers up her trench coat, and swings the other one around. She is wearing a sweater and tartan plaid trousers with laced black sneakers—not quite her usual white Keds, but close. She no longer cares about dressing up for events. Comfort trumps style.

A cold breeze blows in the open car door and I shudder. It is April, and although it was warm and springlike earlier in the day, a chill has settled in the evening air. It seems to take forever for my mom to exit and I grip the steering wheel to control my impatience. This last leg of the trip, dropping off my sister and her son and now my parents, is dragging and I'm getting more agitated with every passing second. I'm anxious for this outing to be over.

When my mom finally steps out, my dad follows quickly behind her. He is one year older than she is, but in better health and more agile. He turns and smiles at me and gives me a pat on my shoulder. His blue-green eyes are watery with fatigue and his thick white hair, which is usually combed neat, is ruffled.

"Will I see you tomorrow?" he asks.

"Yes," I reply. "I can come over after I drop Raymond off at preschool."

I work for my dad as his personal assistant. He officially hired me about six months ago, when his arbitration practice started growing. This arrangement benefits both of us. He needs help with travel arrangements, scheduling, filing, technical support . . . basically everything, and I get to earn a living while still being home with the kids. Although I know I should be thankful for the job, the thought of spending more time with my parents after a day like today causes my chest to tighten and my stomach to drop.

"See you tomorrow," I say as my dad exits the car, and I feel another twist of the key tightening the spring in my chest.

As I pull out of their driveway and head towards home, a ten-minute drive away, I glance in the rearview mirror to make sure Michael is sitting properly in his booster seat. He is staring down at his Pokémon cards so I can't see his face, only the top of his head with its bushy, curly red hair. He looked nice when we started the day but now his white button-down shirt is untucked and stained with lunch and his khaki pants are rumpled. He doesn't appear to care that I'm angry. He never does. My scoldings never seem to have any impact on him, or at least, his behavior never changes. My anger surges again at his indifference.

"Do you know what you did wrong today?" I demand to know.

"Yes," he says without looking up.

"What?" I ask. I want him to say it.

"I kicked you."

It was my parents' idea to take me and my sister Roseann and the two oldest grandchildren, Roseann's six-year-old son, Will, and my four-year-old son, Michael, to see the Broadway show *Mary Poppins*. My dad loves outings in New York City and my mom loves the movie *Mary Poppins*. It seemed like a good idea. Michael had no concept of what it meant to see a musical, but he was excited to hang out with his older cousin.

From the minute I picked up my family to drive to the city I felt uncomfortable, a stressful itch that I only seem to get around my family. Roseann came out of the house looking stylish in gray slacks and a cardigan, her blonde hair blown straight. Roseann is two years older than me. People often think we are twins and yet, around her, I always feel fat, ugly, and disheveled. My own capri pants and button-down blue shirt felt cheap and ill-fitting. My blue tasseled loafers seemed cute when I bought them on sale at Marshall's, but as soon as I put them on outside the store, I realized they are dorky. Plus I don't own a spring coat, so I had to bring my down jacket, which made me feel awkward. I never seem to have the proper clothes. I feel like the whole world looks stylish and I'm always wearing the wrong thing. Even when I try to buy the right thing, like the loafers, I usually get it wrong. That's usually the reason I don't want to go anywhere. If I'm hanging out at home, I can wear jeans and a sweatshirt and feel dressed appropriately. And today, to make matters worse, I had to line my bra with nursing pads so that breast milk didn't leak through my shirt.

Things between Roseann and me have been tense ever since I moved to New Jersey in December, and especially after my daughter, Julia, was born in February. When I moved from Long Island to New Jersey, I had expectations of what it would be like to be closer to my family. I thought my sister and I would hang out all the time, go out to lunch, exercise, and have play-dates with the kids. But she works full time as a lawyer and cannot step away from her desk even for lunch. I also assumed our kids would play together constantly. But her boys are always busy with sports. My feelings are hurt every time I try to make a plan to get together, only to be told Roseann and her family are unavailable. We had an argument after she didn't invite me to Will's school concert.

"I didn't think you'd want to go," she said, her shock and disdain coming through the phone when I asked her why she didn't invite me.

This day in the city was one of the first family events we had after getting over some of our disagreements. Not that we ever resolved any of our disputes. We just pushed the resentments under the rug and hoped we didn't trip over the bump they left.

Michael was fine during the first part of the trip—driving into the city, parking, finding a spot for lunch, and waiting in line to get into the theater. I should have known it was too much to expect a rambunctious four-year-old to sit quietly through a three-hour show. After the intermission, Michael started acting up. He squirmed and repeatedly kicked the seat in front of him. He would not sit still no matter how many times I told him to cut it out. He would turn and make faces at the people behind him and kept flopping around in his chair. I could sense my parents, sitting next to me, getting annoyed. I squeezed his leg and threatened to punish him, but he wouldn't stop. My nephew Will was acting properly, sitting quietly, engaged in the show on the stage.

"He's tired," I whispered to my mom. "He was so excited for today he didn't sleep well last night."

I tried to get him to close his eyes and lean on me but he yelled out, "I'm not tired," disturbing everyone around us. I'd had enough. While Mary Poppins was prancing around the stage and singing "Anything Can Happen," I took him out of the theater. In the lobby he calmed down. We checked out the souvenirs for sale on display in a glass stand. Then he heard the clapping from inside the theater. He realized that the show was over and that he had missed the end. He started screaming at me: "You made me miss the show!" He stamped his feet and threw the program on the floor. "Why did you make me miss the end of the show?"

As the audience emptied out of the theater, Michael continued to scream at me. I was mortified. Even though I wanted Michael to stop, I understood why he was freaking out. His expectations had been built up and the show was boring. Sitting quietly for hours on end was not fun and we had promised him fun.

When we exited the theater onto 42nd street, we were enveloped in the chaos of Times Square. I held Michael's hand as my family weaved their way through the tourists and past the pretzel carts towards the parking garage. I explained again to my family that Michael was so excited about today he didn't sleep well last night and when he's tired, he gets cranky. Then we walked past Ripley's Believe It or Not! Odditorium. Michael got excited at the colorful flashing lights. He wasn't sure what it was, but he knew it was more fun than the show he'd just watched.

"There! I want to go in there! *That's* where I want to go." His four-year-old mind realized that an odditorium was way more fun than a Broadway musical. He tried to pull me across the crowded sidewalk toward the entrance. When I refused and yanked him back toward me, he turned around and kicked me as hard as he could in the shin. My family, who had been a few steps behind us, witnessed the whole scene. Roseann, who had Will's hand in one of her hands, grabbed Michael with her free hand and scolded him.

"You do *not* kick your mother," she said firmly. She held on to him for the rest of the way as we marched through the crowds to the parking garage.

The car ride home from the city was tense. Outside, on the turnpike, the air was thick with white puffy clouds of pollution. Inside the car, the air felt thick with judgment. Michael seemed oblivious to it all. He and Will sat in the way back, playing with Michael's Nintendo DS.

"I'm surprised he didn't fall asleep since he's so tired," my mom said.

Oh, that comment annoyed me. I think about it again as I wait for the train to pass. The train signal lights turn on and the gate arm blocks the intersection. Great, another delay. I look at the clock and realize that Chris won't be home for several hours. He took Ray and Julia to Long Island to visit his mother. He will come back from his family visit with smiles and tales of Nonny's bread and butter cakes made with love. Why can't my family be normal like his? The spring in my chest gets tighter and tighter. I'm sure my parents are talking to each other now about what a horrible child Michael is. And Roseann is telling her husband, Del, how awful it was that Michael kicked me. Why is it always Michael causing problems? Throwing up at the restaurant, breaking the mirrored door at my parents' condo, deflating a blow-up bouncy house. What is wrong with my son that he can't behave? My feelings of insecurity turn to anger at my parents. Normal grandparents would forgive him. Normal grandparents would hug and kiss him and spoil him.

The train passes and the gate rises so that I can continue home. I speak to Michael.

"You know that you behaved very badly Michael, right? You can't kick me. I'm very upset." He doesn't respond.

I sigh and squirm in my seat, feeling awful. I feel twisted inside and just want to crawl in a hole and have everyone, including Michael, go away. Without thinking, I pull into the parking lot of the liquor store, the red one on the corner with an Asian owner. There's a neon Miller Light sign, but I'm not there to buy beer. I leave Michael in the car with strict instructions not to move and I march inside.

I am not thinking. I am not thinking about what it was like before I got pregnant with Julia, when I had started drinking vodka during the day while at home with the boys who, at the time, were three and one and a half. How every day I told myself I wouldn't drink and then I would find myself heading to the liquor store or swiping a bottle from my sister-in-law's house when I was supposed to be feeding her cats. I am not thinking about how I googled "How to control your drinking," but gave up when the only thing that popped up in the search results was a list of AA meetings. I didn't want to stop drinking. I only wanted to stop drinking vodka during the day—but I couldn't. I only stopped when I became pregnant with Julia. But even after I took a pregnancy test and saw the positive results, I waited one day before I told Chris. I gave myself one more night to drink before I committed to the pregnancy and quit drinking for nine months.

I am not thinking about any of this as I find the vodka section in the liquor store. All I know is that I feel awful and there is one thing that I know will make me feel better.

I choose a bottle of Grey Goose because it makes it seem like I'm buying a bottle for company or as a gift for someone.

"Would you like me to gift wrap the bottle?" the clerk asks.

"Yes, please," I respond.

Back in the car, I feel a little better. On the seat next to me is the skinny bottle wrapped in a silver bag and tied with a silver ribbon. We get home. Michael makes a beeline for the couch and turns on the TV. I head to the kitchen and find scissors to cut the ribbon off the bottle. I find a tall glass in the cupboard and fill it a quarter full with vodka. In the fridge I find some lemonade to pour into my glass. I take a sip and the relief is immediate. It is like paint, smoothing over every nick or ragged edge in my psyche. The spring in my chest unwinds and a warm, soft feeling flows through my body. Besides an occasional beer now and then, I haven't had anything to drink since the night I took the pregnancy test almost a year ago. My tolerance is low and the buzz happens quickly.

I put the bottle in our liquor cabinet. Not being a drinker, Chris never looks in there and even if he does, it would be normal for us to have a bottle of Grey Goose for guests. I plop down on the couch with Michael and say I'm sorry that we got into a fight. We hug and everything seems better. Chris calls to say he is leaving Huntington now and to report that Julia is refusing a bottle. Shit, I was afraid of that. I had been nursing her and slacking off on giving her a bottle. The boys had been able to take both with no issues. But I just didn't have the time to introduce the bottle to Julia. I have two more hours before they come home and before my two-month-old reaches for my breast to nurse. *I can pump and dump the tainted breast milk in time*, I promise myself, and I pour another drink.

ESCAPE FOR THE NIGHT

December 28, 2010
Eleven days until sober

One morning, during Christmas break, Roseann calls to ask for my help scanning and sending a document. I'm often the tech support for my family, not because I'm tech-savvy but because I take the time to read the directions. Chris is home with the kids, so I drive over to my sister's, happy to have an excuse to get out of the house. I wasn't planning on telling her what was going on between me and Chris and my drinking problem, but when I see her, it all comes pouring out of me. My affair, Chris's finding out, how I learned about Chris's extramarital relationships, and how I have been drinking vodka during the day. Roseann is surprised by my story, but not as shocked as I thought she'd be. It feels good to tell someone, speak my concerns out loud, if only to get them out of my head temporarily.

Roseann gets up from her computer and I follow her down two flights of stairs from her attic office into the kitchen, passing my three nephews who are sprawled out on the living room couch watching TV. She makes her lunch while I explain that Chris and I need to figure out what we are going to do. I guess we'll go to a marriage counselor. Maybe we'll separate.

"How can you guys even have a conversation with the kids always around?" she asks.

"We can't really," I say. "It's been difficult. And sometimes we get in bad fights in front of them." I whisper so my nephews don't hear.

She focuses on the fact that Chris and I need to talk away from the kids and offers to watch them for the night so that he and I can really sit down and hash it all out. I thank her for the offer.

"I'll ask Chris," I say, "but I'm not sure he wants to be alone with me for the night." When I come home, the kids are playing Wii in the living room.

"Where's Dad?" I ask. They shrug.

I find him in the basement doing laundry. Lately, Chris has been doing all the laundry. Sometimes I'm a little suspicious because it means he spends a lot of time alone in the basement. Is he down here because he's texting Robin? On the flip side, it's nice to have the laundry washed and folded.

As Chris looks through a wicker bin of mismatched socks, I tell him about Roseann's offer, that she said she'd take the kids for the night so that we could talk.

"Really?" he says, looking up from the sock bin, his eyes bright. "When can we drop them off?"

"Well," I stammer. "I didn't tell her we would yet. I wasn't sure you'd want to . . ." I feel stupid for not immediately taking Roseann up on her offer. In my defense, Chris hasn't been talking to me, much less acting like he wants to spend time alone with me.

"Why would we turn down a night away from the kids? Call her back and say we'll drop them off in an hour." While I call Roseann from our house phone, Chris gets on his cell and reserves a room at the Ocean Place Resort & Spa, a large hotel located on the beach. It's the hotel where we spent our wedding night.

"Let's get massages," he says when I hang up with Roseann. He is staring at me expectantly with his large dark eyes. It's the first time he's looked at me in two weeks.

"Okay," I say hesitantly. "But I thought we are going to talk about us." Chris says we need to take advantage of my sister's offer. We both laugh at the notion that it takes us almost divorcing to get someone to watch the kids for the night. We head upstairs to tell the kids to pack an overnight bag. They are super excited to spend the night with their cousins. Chris and I are excited to be kid-free for a night.

While Chris checks us in, I sit on the round chair in the lobby. The chair was once white but now looks beige and dingy. The rug also looks dirty and stained, and I notice how the whole lobby looks tired and worn. It's been nine years since we were here for our wedding night and it looks as if the owner hasn't made any attempt at upkeep for the hotel.

We put our bags in our room and immediately head to the spa for our massages. We are a little early for our scheduled appointments, so we hang out in the waiting area in our bathrobes and sip lemon water. When it's my turn, I tell the masseuse that I don't really like massages because I'm always cold, so she puts electric warmers on my hands and feet. It's lovely and I feel relaxed.

After the massages, we hang out for a bit in the hot tub. The gurgling of the bubbles acts like a white noise machine, blocking the disturbing thoughts in my head. I'm enjoying Chris's company instead of focusing on the rolling list of mistakes he has made. I take a break from wondering if our marriage will survive.

"This was a good idea, Chris," I say. "Thanks."

Back in the room, we shower and then climb into the huge king-sized bed naked. It feels luxurious to be napping in the middle of the afternoon. After we make love, we laugh about our wedding night. I was sick with a nasty head cold and had lost my voice. Chris had what we dubbed "limo leg." He'd pulled a thigh muscle getting in and out of the limo. On our wedding night, we limped and collapsed into bed. We didn't consummate the marriage until the next morning.

That was a lifetime ago. Now we have fucked up everything we promised to each other nine years ago. But we don't talk about any of that. We have an unspoken agreement to put it all on a shelf for the night. We can take it back down in the morning. Tonight we do something we should have done six months ago: we pay attention to each other. We try to remember the last time we went away. It was probably when I was pregnant with Julia and we went to the Grand Canyon for a friend's wedding. That was three years ago.

Tonight's escape is wonderful, but beneath our laughs and tenderness is an underground river of shit that neither of us want to plunge into just yet. We don't even want to stick our toes in for fear we will get swept away.

The next morning, when I go to pick the kids up from my sister's, I can't meet Roseann's gaze.

"Did you guys talk?" she asks.

"Yes," I say. "Thank you so much. Nothing is settled but it was good to have a night without the kids. Thanks so much," I repeat.

That week, Chris immediately plans another weekend away. For that trip, I employ our babysitter Bethany to watch the kids for the weekend.

WHAT HAPPENED . . .

WHAT HAPPENED . . .

WHAT HAPPENED . . .

WHAT HAPPENED . . .

WHAT HAPPENED . . .

FIRST AA MEETING

December 30, 2010
Nine days until sober

I glance at the oven to check the time: 6:20 p.m. Almost time to go. I pick up Michael's wet gloves, which had been left on the floor by the back door, and hang them on the kitchen chair to dry. In the downstairs bathroom, the unrenovated, crappy old one that Chris and I use, I wash my face and brush my teeth. I think about changing out of what I'm wearing, jeans and a sweatshirt, but I quickly dismiss that. This is the best I can do today. My hair has slipped out of its ponytail, so I redo it, pulling it tight to get all the hair out of my face. The kids are in the living room watching *Pokémon*. I should go sit with them for a minute. Snuggle in on the couch and reassure them that their mom is still here. But I just can't. Instead I go sit on the edge of my bed.

What am I going to do now? is the constant question bouncing around my head. How is this going to work? One of us will have to move out, but can we even afford that? I have no money of my own. A wave of helplessness washes over me. I can't stay and I can't leave. I want to drink. I want vodka to wash everything away. The realization that I can no longer drink hits me like a battering ram in the gut and I bend over from the impact of the need and the loss.

I grab my purse from the bedroom floor, brushing off a dust bunny that had gotten stuck to it. I search inside for the business card from MaryAnne, the alcoholism counselor I saw last week. On the back of the card she wrote: "7 p.m. Thursday Women's Step meeting, United Methodist Church, Red Bank." My therapist, Michelle, sent me to MaryAnne. MaryAnne told me to go to this women's AA meeting. I do whatever anyone tells me to do because I don't know what else to do. I don't know how to fix this. I learn later, at a meeting, that this is called "the Gift of Desperation."

I hear the back door open and Chris banging his boots against the house to knock off the snow. I get up out of my daze. I find my jacket and tell Chris I'm going. He's inside the kitchen, peeling off his wet jacket and snow pants. There is steam coming off his sweaty head. He barely acknowledges that I've talked to him, but I know he hears me. Usually he gets angry if I depart without saying goodbye. A proper "goodbye" with a kiss. When we were first married, I had to be trained to do this because it wasn't something my family did or cared about. If you left, then you were gone. No one's feelings were hurt because you didn't make a big fuss out of saying goodbye. That's not so in Chris's family. You must say hello and goodbye with a kiss. I find it exhausting. In the living room, I pause and try to connect with the kids.

"I'm going out for a bit. I'll be back in about an hour." Michael ignores me, engrossed in the show. Julia and Ray turn and smile at me.

"Where you going, Momma?" Julia asks.

"Just out to see some friends for coffee. I'll be back soon." One day soon I will tell them where I go and why I need to go there, but today's not the day for that. With a smile and a wave, I head out the door.

Earlier in the day, Chris cleared the snow off the minivan. He still takes care of me, even though he's so furious that he refuses to look at me. As I reverse out of the driveway, I note how nice our newly renovated Cape looks. From the outside things look cozy, sweet with a fresh coat of snow and a twinkling Christmas tree in the window. You'd never guess that inside a family is falling apart.

It's 6:45 p.m. when the minivan's tires crunch on the snowy church parking lot. I'm early as usual. Sitting in the parked car, I notice my knuckles are white from gripping the steering wheel. I stretch out my fingers. My skin is so dry, I'm tempted to lick my palms. I rummage in my purse for hand cream that doesn't exist. Normal thirty-eight-year-old women carry moisturizer in their purses. Not disorganized fuckups like me. I call Kelly to confirm that she and Scott are coming for dinner tomorrow. Normally we spend New Year's Eve at Kelly's ski house in Vermont but no one, especially me and Chris, can make that happen this year.

"I'm about to go into my first AA meeting," I tell her.

"I'm proud of you," Kelly says. My face flushes with shame. Proud? The other day I retrieved a half-empty bottle of vodka from the garbage can. There is nothing to be proud of here. I mumble thanks and goodbye.

I hear the *click-clack* of high-heeled boots on pavement and glance in the rearview mirror. A youngish, blond-haired woman walks at a fast clip toward the church. She's wearing a long, puffy, black jacket and carrying a huge orange Coach bag. I bet she has hand cream in her purse. I exit my car and follow behind her, giving her a large lead so she won't be tempted to turn and talk to me.

We go into the church through the back door, down the stairs, around several corners. Tethered to this woman by an invisible rope; I am pulled into a room. Dusty old couches and ripped armchairs line the walls. A few women are seated, chit-chatting. I make a beeline to a chair flanked by empty seats. When I'm settled, I look up, and across from me is Orange Coach Bag. She smiles, munching on Oreos. I avert my eyes.

The room fills up quickly, and now there are no empty seats. At exactly 7:00 p.m., a woman speaks.

"Welcome to the Thursday night Women's Step meeting. Let's begin by saying the 'Serenity Prayer.'" My hands are clenched again, and I stare at them while the other women pray in unison. I mumble along, pretending I know the words. After the prayer, the leader reads a list of things I don't understand. It's like she's speaking a different language. When her list is over, she says, "Let's introduce ourselves." I knew this part was coming. From movies and TV shows. Maybe from the one Al-Anon meeting I attended as a teen.

My heart pounds and my armpits dampen. Like counting down the seconds on a clock, the introductions tick toward me.

"Mary, Alcoholic." Tick. Three away.

"Hi, I'm Susan, I'm an alcoholic." Tick. Two away.

"Lauren, Alcoholic." Tick and I'm next. Then something surprising happens. The words float easily out of my mouth. "Hi. I'm Liz and I'm an alcoholic." I exhale and lean back into the worn armchair.

After the introductions, the leader says they are discussing Step One. How are they only on Step One? They go around the room again. Most of what they say is foreign, but every so often a snippet makes sense. One woman talks about how she'd tell her husband she was going to the pharmacy but instead she'd go to the liquor store and drink in the parking lot. I can relate. One woman says she had trouble admitting she had a drinking problem because she managed to go to work every day, albeit hungover and miserable. I can relate. Terror grips me when I realize, once again, it will be my turn.

A middle-aged woman sitting next to Orange Coach Bag says she is so happy to be at a meeting. *Happy to be at an AA meeting? Happy that you can no longer drink?* I'm baffled.

She says she is thankful for the tools that got her through the holidays and the snowstorm. She ends with, "I'm so grateful to be a sober mom today." The phrase "sober mom" echoes in my head. Something about these two words strung together cracks me open. Tears stream down my face. I try to control them because now it's my turn to speak.

In a shaky voice, I manage to say something about it being my first meeting. I can't stop drinking. My life is falling apart. My husband and I might be separating. I can't say anything else because now I'm sobbing. My body shakes. Tears and snot drip down my face. One woman hands me a tissue and another pats my back. This makes me cry harder. The next thing I know we're standing, and everyone holds hands and says the "Our Father." I find it odd that they are saying such a Christian prayer, but I'm grateful I know this one. The meeting is over.

I wipe my face with the tissue. Putting my head down, I bolt for the door, but my exit is blocked by a semicircle of women. Each one smiles and says, "Welcome." One hugs me. They ask for my number and punch it into their phones. Orange Coach Bag says, "You never have to feel this way again."

I walk outside and inhale the cold, crisp air. The clouds are gone and a thick crescent moon hovers in the night sky. Nothing has changed but everything feels different. I couldn't name what I was feeling at the time. It'd be months before I could identify my feelings. But now I know what it was. It was hope. Walking back to the car, I repeat my new mantra in my head: "Sober mom. Sober mom."

WHEN A MAN LOVES A WOMAN

"Once more: The alcoholic at certain times has no effective mental defense against the first drink."

—"More About Alcoholism," *Alcoholics Anonymous* [1]

January 7, 2011
One day until sober

I wake up as usual, five minutes before the 6:00 a.m. alarm. I hear the sound of the coffee maker, preset the night before, brewing. Chris is stirring next to me. As the fog of sleep slowly disperses, I remember: *Shit! I drank last night.* The realization jolts me awake; I pop out of bed and run to the kitchen. I scan the room to make sure there is no evidence of this fact. Relief washes over me when I see that everything looks normal. Last night I ran the dishwasher, wiped down the counters. I remember now that I hid the bottle of vodka in the closet, in my brown leather boots. As I pull the coffee cups out from the cupboard, I replay last night's events. What happened? Why did I drink?

Last night was Wednesday, Chris's studio night, which meant after work he went straight to Long Island to jam with his friends. They smoke pot and play Dead tunes. And I did what I would normally do. Before my deck confession to Chris. Before I went to an alcoholism counselor. Before I attended my first AA meeting and raised my hand and admitted to a group of strangers I was an alcoholic. When I went to the grocery store on my way home from work, I got $20 cash back with my purchase. After school I took the kids to the park. Then, on our way home, we went through the McDonald's drive-thru for a dinner of chicken nuggets and french fries. While the kids waited in the car, I ran into the liquor store and picked up a bottle of Svedka vodka. The size that costs just under $20. I paid with cash. There was no pause. No AA person blocking my path. Nothing I had learned in the meeting stopped me from walking straight into the store and buying vodka.

The kids ate dinner and I poured myself a drink: half vodka, half cranberry juice. I took a sip, closed my eyes, and exhaled. My body and mind welcomed their old friend. For a moment, the stress of the past month disappeared. I turned up the radio and danced while cleaning up the dinner mess.

The rest of the night was uneventful. I didn't drink so much that I threw up or blacked out. Just enough to fill the emptiness. Just enough to feel like myself. I texted Chris a nice loving message telling him to enjoy himself. Things have been okay between us lately. Not perfect but okay. I got the kids in bed, helping Julia pick out an outfit for her first day of preschool.

All this comes back to me as I pour myself and Chris a cup of coffee. Milk for me, milk and sugar for him. I didn't leave the vodka out on the counter but Chris might still somehow know I drank. He might have smelled it on me when he came home from the studio. I need to test his mood this morning. I place his coffee on his nightstand, kiss him on the forehead, and get back in bed with my coffee. And I wait. Chris mumbles thank you and gets up to go to the bathroom. I'm sitting in the bed sipping my coffee when he returns. I meet his eyes.

"How was your night?"

"Oh, great. We worked on that new song." He proceeds to tell me about the mixing board setup and the recording they've been working on. He doesn't know I drank. I exhale, realizing I had been holding my breath. I smile and tell him the kids and I had a boring night. Julia was cute picking out her outfit for her first day of preschool today. We chitchat as we begin our morning routine. Chris leaves for work, I take the kids to school.

After the school drop-off I walk into the house, wiping the slush off my hiking boots on the rug by the front door. I head into the kitchen to make a fresh pot of coffee. As I wait for the coffee to brew, I rinse out the cereal bowls and put them in the dishwasher. I grab the dustpan from the closet and sweep up the flakes of cereal scattered underneath the kids' chairs. *Do they get any in their mouths?* I grumble to myself.

I note how quiet it is. For weeks, because of the renovation, construction guys were constantly in and out of the house. Then Chris and the kids were home for winter break. This is the first time I've been alone in the house for weeks, maybe months. I soak up the quiet, breathe, and sip my coffee.

My Blackberry beeps. Chris wants to know how Julia did at drop-off. I text him back that she was fine—no tears, excited to start school. Julia turns three in February but the teachers at Ray's preschool agreed to let her start in the three-year-old class in January. Of course they agreed; it's more money for them, and their school's enrollment has been low. For me, it means that three days a week I have 9:00 a.m. to noon with no kids. I haven't had this much kid-free time since before Michael was born. The goal is to give me more time to work. My administrative assistant job for my father continues to grow, and it has been a struggle to get work done and watch the kids. But right now, my father is away at a conference in New York City, Chris is at work, and the kids are at school. I have a moment to pause and think.

My mind goes to the bottle of vodka hidden in my brown leather riding boots in the back of my closet. A rising tide of anxiety brews in my stomach. I drank; now what? I'm supposed to go to a meeting tonight. What do I tell them? Why did I drink last night? And if I drank last night, why the fuck did I not drink through Christmas and New Year's? I really could have used a drink to get through those horrible holidays.

Christmas Eve dinner with Chris's family at a restaurant in Long Island was torture. No one would talk to me except Chris's brother-in-law Rainer. A former psychoanalyst, he gave me marriage advice, but all I could concentrate on was the gin and tonic he was sipping.

New Year's Eve was no better. Kelly and Scott drove down from North Jersey to hang with us. Such good friends, they knew our marriage is falling apart and were kind enough to just be there for us. Not wanting to make the whole not-drinking thing weird, I insisted they bring beer, which of course made it weird. Scott told me later that my insistence made him upset. He hadn't wanted to drink in front of me, but I forced him.

We ordered pizza and sat around our cramped living room while the kids played in the basement. Chris strummed his guitar while we made small talk. Pain and hurt radiated off of Chris and I was an empty vessel of nothingness. There were a couple of jokes about what an awful year it was. Kelly and Scott didn't stay until midnight. The next morning I was so proud of myself for making it through New Year's without drinking.

But now here I am again. I drank when I said I wouldn't. Although nothing terrible happened. I didn't get in a car accident or get a DWI. I didn't neglect the kids. I still showed up for work. Maybe I'm blowing this whole drinking thing out of proportion. Chris gets to smoke pot with his friends. Why can't I drink? I'm supposed to go to the women's AA meeting tonight. Will I have to tell them I drank? Certainly I will have to tell MaryAnne, the alcoholism counselor, on Friday. I decide I hate the counselor, with her bleach-blond hair and her freezing cold annex office and her insistence on talking about my mother. She was the one who told me to go to the Thursday women's meeting and I did feel better after attending it. The meeting quieted my brain for an hour. I listened to other people instead of thinking about myself or what would become of me and Chris. I was intrigued by the specific language in the meeting and its rituals, even though I didn't understand them yet. In a way, the meetings remind me of church: you never want to go but you always feel better after attending.

For some reason a movie pops into my head. An old one in which Meg Ryan is a stay-at-home spouse who can't stop drinking. The husband is a pilot. What is that movie called? I google Meg Ryan movies and learn it's *When a Man Loves a Woman*. Maybe if I watch that movie I'll figure out this drinking thing. What to do. How to stop. Or rather how to control my drinking. It's available on Netflix. I decide to watch it. I've got nothing to do at the moment, no work for my dad, and the kids are all at school. This will be research.

It feels so decadent to watch a movie in an empty house at ten in the morning. There is Meg Ryan drinking and having fun with her pilot husband, played by Andy García. At one point he scolds her, "It's getting less fun to wring you out at the end of the night." She agrees and promises to cut back. But there she is, drinking vodka during the day. I pause the movie. Without a thought, I grab the Svedka vodka out of my brown leather riding boots, go to the kitchen, and make myself a vodka cranberry.

I continue to watch the movie. Meg Ryan looks so pretty fishing her vodka bottle out of the garbage in her nightgown. I've done that, several times. Although I wear pajamas, not nightgowns. I finish watching the movie, crying at the appropriate parts. I don't quite understand it all but I'm enjoying the buzz I have from the vodka. I feel like myself again. I've been so uncomfortable since December, like there are tiny razors inside of me. And now the razors have retracted.

Chris calls and we chat.

"Are you going to a meeting tonight?" he asks.

"Nah, I don't feel like it tonight," I say. Once I took a sip of my drink, I made the decision not to attend the Thursday Women's Step meeting.

Chris is annoyed. He went to great lengths to switch his studio nights from Thursday nights to Wednesday nights so that I could attend this meeting.

I drink a cup of coffee before I have to pick up Julia and Ray from preschool. Then I brush my teeth and spritz some fragrance on me, so I don't smell like vodka. I'm able to act normal at preschool pickup. The teachers tell me that Julia did well on her first day. We all knew she would. Back at home, the kids and I wait for the bus to drop off Michael. After they have an after-school snack, I pour myself another drink. While I make meatloaf for dinner, I keep a glass of vodka cranberry behind the cookie jar.

The front door opens and Chris comes in. He greets the kids and then walks into the kitchen to kiss me hello. Immediately I can tell he knows I've been drinking. *Now?* I think in frustration. All those other times he never noticed, but now he can tell? After dinner he sits me down at the kitchen table.

"Have you been drinking?"

"Yes." I'm astonished at my honest answer. "I don't know why. I'm sorry." My voice shakes, my eyes tear.

"I ask that if you drink in the future that you don't drive with the kids in the car," he says calmly.

"Okay," I say. "But I'm not going to drink anymore."

It's a very adult conversation. There is no yelling from him.

"I won't drink again," I repeat. I hear myself and I wince. I sound like a stereotypical alcoholic. I hate myself. A stay-at-home mother who drinks vodka during the day and then promises she won't drink again. It's pathetic. Even Meg Ryan can't make this look glamorous.

The next day I go to MaryAnne, the alcoholism counselor. When she asks if I drank, I nod "yes." She's not surprised. On Wednesday I go to my therapist, Michelle. I tell her I drank again. She is not surprised. On Thursday, I attend the Women's Step meeting that I skipped the previous week because I was drunk. After the meeting, I tell the two women who always ask how I'm doing that I drank. No one is surprised or upset with me.

FINDING A SPONSOR

January 13, 2011
Five days sober

In a semicircle around me, the women from the Thursday night meeting say to me:

"Do you have a Big Book?"

"Do you have a sponsor?"

"Do you have a home group?"

"Can't this be my home group?" I ask. I like this Thursday night Women's Step meeting. I'm familiar with it, comfortable around these women. But they tell me no. It's not a home group. *What the fuck is a home group?* They see my confusion and one says, "A home group is a meeting with a secretary, where they record your sober date and you celebrate your anniversaries. You'll get a commitment." *Just what I need*, I think, *another commitment. Being stretched too thin is part of my problem.*

The women enthusiastically tell me about other meetings. There's Friday mornings in Fair Haven. That's a good meeting. And the Candlelight Beginners' meeting on Mondays in Red Bank. Saturday night Open Speaker meeting. *Why do these meetings sound like bars or nightclubs?* They are talking at me rapid-fire and I'm getting overwhelmed. I glance at the door.

"Does anyone have a meeting book?" someone asks the group. Several people look around the room as if a meeting book, whatever that is, will miraculously appear on one of the worn couches. I'm not going to remember the dates and times of all these meetings. My brain is a sieve lately. Finally, a short woman with tattoos tells me there is a website that lists all the meetings.

"Google it," she says, "It's called AA North Jersey."

"But we live in Central Jersey," I respond. She looks at me strangely.

"Okay, I'll check that out," I promise, relieved to have a way to check and double-check the meeting's time and location. I don't do "wing it" well.

Orange Coach Bag, whose name I've learned is Mary, tells me she is going to Sunday night five o'clock at Tower Hill and that I should go. She is a few years younger than me, with straight blond hair and glasses. We look alike except she is dressed in nicer clothes. My brain scans our weekend calendar. I don't think we have anything scheduled. Just another weekend stuck in the house with the anger and tension.

"I'll try to come," I tell Mary.

I can't fully commit to anything. My life has been upheaved. It's like a laundry basket of clean clothes dumped on the bed in a big heap, waiting to be folded. It's overwhelming and there's nowhere to sit until the mess is cleaned up.

That night, after I put the kids to bed, I tell Chris, "I'm supposed to go to more meetings. Apparently one a week is not enough. Some people go to a meeting every day." I can tell by Chris's face that he is annoyed, but he says, "Whatever you gotta do." He's been going to Al-Anon. I'm not sure what they've been telling him, but he has had a more hands-off attitude lately. Not like the time he called my therapist Michelle. She wouldn't even get on the phone with him. The receptionist said curtly, "Michelle recommends you talk to your own therapist." Oh, he was pissed! He claims he was calling to clarify something she said in our one unplanned joint therapy session. But I'm pretty sure he was calling to see if she could provide any insight into my mind. This seems to be what's driving him most crazy; he can't read my thoughts. He asks me questions and I answer him honestly, but he doesn't know that. He just found out that I've been lying to him for years, secretly drinking. And then I had an affair. Why should he believe anything I say now?

"I think I'm going to stop seeing MaryAnne," I say. "She's not really helping me." MaryAnne is the alcoholism counselor who focuses every session on my mother.

He is nonchalant again. "Whatever you think is best." I'm annoyed by this detachedness. I don't want him to care, but I also want him to engage. He is giving me the cold shoulder, something I used to try to give him back in our days at the College Board.

I walk away from him and go into our office. Our Ikea desk is scattered with papers—the kids' schoolwork and my boss's/father's case documents that I need to work on. *One day, I'll get this organized*, I promise to myself. I log on to my side of the computer and pull up Amazon.com. I search for "Big Book," and "Alcoholics Big Book" appears in my search field. Scanning the search results, I note that the "Big Book" is actually called *Alcoholics Anonymous*. Years later, in meetings, I'll hear that the Big Book is the book most stolen from libraries.

Amazon suggests other related topics:

Alcoholism recovery
Twelve-Step programs

Health, fitness, and dieting
Substance abuse recovery

A book cover pops up in the side advertisements. Should I buy a book cover for this book? I don't plan on walking around with it.

Once again I cringe at the cliché I am. The drunk mom. I'm an embarrassment. Thank God I can order this book anonymously from the Internet without the mortification of having to ask a Barnes & Noble store clerk where the self-help section is.

I have options for the Big Book. There's a paperback, a hardcover, and an accompanying workbook. I click on the most inconspicuous one, a blue paperback edition that looks like a bible. In the future, I learn it's better to buy a hardcover because it's more difficult to throw away.

There, I mutter to myself, after completing the purchase. I've done one thing for sobriety. My spirits lift a little. The book will arrive in a couple of days. I quickly check my Yahoo account for emails from my boss/father. I have been disconnected from my job lately, and I worry he is noticing my distance. Because of my therapy appointments, I had to tell him I'm not available on Wednesday afternoons and Thursday mornings. I'm waiting for him to tell me I need to step up my game at work, but so far he hasn't said anything. Bethany, the babysitter, comes on Tuesdays, and I try to keep that day of the week solely for work. The rest of the week, I do work when I can squeeze it in—after the kids go to bed or while they are watching TV before and after school.

I shut down the computer, climb into bed, and wait for Chris to join me. Having done that one thing for my recovery, buying the Big Book, makes me feel better. Maybe I will be able to do all those things the women were telling me I need to do.

January 16, 2011
Eight days sober

Sunday comes and Chris wants to go to Long Island to visit his family. I remind him of my plans to go to the five o'clock meeting, but say that I can skip it if he thinks I should come. He says it's fine. He'll go without me. I'm glad to have time to myself but I'm worried about what Chris's family thinks of me. They know I'm an alcoholic and I'm sure they are all talking about me behind my back. I want to come along on the visit to Long Island to show them that I'm normal. "I'm fine. You don't need to worry about me!" But I've said I would meet Mary at the five o'clock meeting, so that's what I should do. I'm learning accountability.

With the house empty, I spend the morning cleaning. I decide to tackle my closet. Lately I've been shoving stuff in there and it's a mess. I pull everything out and drop it in a big heap in the middle of the office so I can go through it and put it in piles—toss, give away, or keep—like they do on those home improvement shows.

As I pull stuff out, I spot a plastic bottle of Svedka vodka tossed in the back. Shame floods my body like warm water, starting at my toes and moving up to my face until I'm drowning in it. Something about the plastic bottle feels even more humiliating than a glass bottle. Cheap and trashy.

I wish Chris were here to see the bottle, because he still has a hard time believing that I drank so much behind his back. Here is proof, but he's not here to witness it. And now what do I do with this bottle? If he sees it in the recycling, he'll think I drank today while he was away visiting his family. It's probably what he expects I'll do. I wonder too if a part of him wants me to drink again. It'll prove I am the fuckup he thinks I am.

If I wrap the plastic bottle in paper towels and shove it deep in the trash, like I used to do, and he sees it, he will definitely not believe that it's an old bottle after I took the pains to hide it. Plus, that's dishonest, right? We've agreed to be 100 percent honest with each other going forward. I have no other choice but to be up-front with him when he gets home. I squirm at the thought of the future discussion. Will he believe me that this is a discarded old bottle I found while cleaning my closet?

My cell phone rings and I see it is Mary, Orange Coach Bag. I don't pick up. It's nice that she is calling but I have nothing to say to her. I don't even know her and she doesn't know me. Plus, I'm planning on going to the meeting this afternoon. She said she'd be there. I'll see her then.

Organizing the closet is a big project and I lose my oomph about halfway through. I end up neatly piling the stuff back in the closet.

Now what? The house is so quiet. There is so much more I could be doing, like cleaning the bathrooms or finding curtains for the kitchen window, but I'm exhausted and have lost all energy to do anything. Now would be when I would have a drink. It would give me a brief burst of energy to finish a project, and then make me sleepy enough to take a quick nap. I should go for a walk but instead I curl up in a fetal position on my side of the bed and stare out the window at the trees in the neighbor's yard. From this vantage point, I don't see the ugly split-level house across the street with the pickup truck parked in the grass next to the house. All I see are tall, slender trees swaying in the breeze against a backdrop of blue sky.

I lay like that for twenty minutes. I'm unable to fall asleep but I feel the anxiety release from my body as I lay there. Finally I get up, shower, get dressed, and drive to the church where the meeting is held. It's a church I'm familiar with, one I attended occasionally with a childhood friend when I'd sleep over at her house. All these meetings secretly happening in all these churches all over town. It amuses me.

When I sit down and the meeting begins, a now-familiar feeling washes over me. The "Serenity Prayer" signals my brain. Shut down. Relax. Listen to what the speakers are saying. I don't think about Chris and my mistakes and how I'm a drunk mom cliché. I sit back and listen to the speakers. After the meeting, Mary introduces me to Joy, another blonde, but shorter and with an athletic build.

"This is the woman I was telling you about," Mary says to Joy. *They've been talking about me?* I don't like being the subject of a conversation between these women. They don't even know me. Joy is very enthusiastic. She is pretty and well-put-together. It comes up that I'm a mother, and she is delighted.

"Me too!" she says. "I have three kids: a six-year-old, a five-year-old, and a three-year-old."

"I have three too. Six, four, and two. Wait, no that's wrong. They are seven, five, and almost three." My faces flushes hot. *Oh my God, what will she think of me? A mother who doesn't know the ages of her own children?* Joy doesn't seem to notice the gaffe. She goes on to tell me she hosts a meeting at her house on Thursday mornings. Kids are welcome. Like every other woman in AA, we exchange numbers.

One week goes by and I don't call Joy. My kids are both in school on Thursdays, and for some reason I think I can't attend her house meeting unless the kids come. So, the following week, I make a plan to pull the kids out of school so we can all go to Joy's home meeting. In hindsight this plan is ridiculous; why would I pull the kids out of school to attend a meeting? But at the time it seemed totally logical. I wouldn't have been able to tell you at the time but I felt drawn to this meeting. It seemed important that I attend. Maybe because Joy was the first mom I met in AA who had kids the same age as mine. But it was also because Joy had an energy I was attracted to. She was smart—a no-nonsense type with a sharp wit.

Tuesday, January 25, 2011
Seventeen days sober

On Tuesday I drop my kids off at preschool and then, while sitting in the preschool parking lot, I call Joy. I tell her I plan to come on Thursday, and that I'll bring my two youngest. She says "great," and gives me her address, which I write down in the back of the Big Book. Later, when I find the penciled-in address scribbled in the back of my book, I'm filled with a nostalgic sense of awe. This chicken scratch is a like a caveman painting: an ancient sign of when things were much different and were about to change drastically.

Thursday, January 27, 2011
Nineteen days sober

On Thursday I get the kids ready, making sure they are in semi-acceptable clothing. We load into the car and I follow the Google directions to Joy's home. Much to my relief it's a small Cape, even smaller than my own home. I wouldn't have been able to deal if it had been one of these huge, well-appointed houses. At least this woman isn't super rich. I'm tired of feeling like everyone is more together than me.

There are only four of us at the meeting. This is the smallest meeting I've been to. I learn later that a meeting can have just two people. The meeting's format is new to me. Sitting around Joy's kitchen table, we read a page from the *Daily Meditations* and then share on that topic. Today's reflections is: "Serving my brother. The member talks to the newcomer not in a spirit of power but in a spirit of humility and weakness."[1] When it's my turn to share, I shrug and say I can't really comment, having only two weeks of sobriety myself. I am the newcomer. But Joy balks at this answer.

"There are people in the meetings with one day or even hours sober. You've got two weeks! You can help them." *What could I possibly offer anyone*, I think. *My life is a disaster.*

The meeting ends and one women leaves. The other, I learn, is Joy's sponsee and lives in North Jersey. I explain to Joy what's going on with me, how my marriage is falling apart, how it's so difficult to be in the house with Chris.

"Do you have a sponsor?" she asks. I tell her that I did ask a woman from the Thursday night meeting.

"Are you working the steps?" Joy asks.

"No, I don't know what that means." She shakes her head slightly. She is disappointed at something. I can't tell if it's me or something else.

"Well, the way I was told to do it: I call my sponsor every day and, in the beginning, we meet once a week to do step work. And I go to her home group so I can see her in person at least once a week."

"My sponsor didn't tell me any of that."

"Well, that's just how my sponsor does it and what I do with my sponsees."

"Well then," I stammer, feeling like a nervous child. "Can you be my sponsor?" I cringe at the desperation in my voice. The other woman laughs. "Joy is the best! She is a great sponsor."

Joy agrees to be my sponsor but tells me I need to call the other woman and tell her I'm going to "work with someone else." *Work?* I think. *What work are we doing?* I insist that the woman is not going to miss me. I haven't talked to her in over a week.

The first thing Joy tells me is that I need to join her home group. It's on Wednesday nights at eight in the evening at Christ Church in Shrewsbury. Yet another meeting in yet another church. I tell her no, sorry, I can't go Wednesdays because it's Chris's studio night.

"Well, ask him if he can change," Joy says matter-of-factly. "We can't be afraid to ask for things. He can always say 'no,' but you never know, it might not be a big deal to change it back again."

This is a big deal, I think. Once a week, Chris meets with his friends to play music and get high. I don't tell Joy about the getting high part. But I do tell her that he just switched his studio night from Thursday to Wednesday so that I could go to that Women's Step meeting once a week. She frowns a little at the mention of the Women's Step meeting. I can tell she doesn't approve of that meeting, but I don't know why. It seems like I will never figure out the ins and outs of AA.

"Well, it's one of my requirements," she says. Actually, she doesn't say "requirements." But that's the message that comes through. I will learn that Joy has an amazing way of telling you what to do without actually telling you what to do. She does it by talking about her experience. How her sponsor insisted Joy go to her home group and what a pain it had been but how she went every week no matter what, even when she was pregnant and afterwards when she had a newborn. And now she never misses home group. How she even bought her house because it's so close to her home group. She could walk! She explains, "I expect my sponsees to have the same home group as me so that I can see them once a week and we can check in. Just talk to him," she insists, "and explain the situation." The last thing she says is, "Call me every day."

"Oh," I respond. "I'm going away for the weekend with Chris. I will call you when I get back."

"Oh, are you not an alcoholic on the weekends?"

I feel stupid. Of course I am. I'm a fucking alcoholic every fucking day.

"Call me every day to check in, no matter if you are home or away."

I load the kids up into the minivan and pull away from her house. Again, just like when I ordered the Big Book, I feel lighter. I've done something for my sobriety. Maybe I can do this. Maybe I can quit drinking.

Later that day, Chris and I excuse the kids from dinner, and they run into the living room to watch *Ben 10.* As we rinse the dinner dishes and put them in the dishwasher, Chris tells me about a fight brewing at work regarding an upcoming conference. Chris has left the College Board and now works for a different nonprofit membership organization. The honeymoon period at his new job is over and now I hear about the assholes at work who are giving him headaches. When he is finished, I tell Chris that I've gotten a new sponsor. I describe Joy. She's got three kids, two girls and a boy Julia's age, she lives in a small Cape, her husband is a doctor. She's been sober seven years. He is genuinely happy for me and gives me a hug. I grip him tightly, knowing the next thing I say won't make him as happy.

"She wants me to go to her home group on Wednesday nights."

"But you already go to a meeting on Monday and Thursday nights."

"I'll have to switch Thursday with Wednesday. Plus, Alice and Mary go to a meeting every night. Some people go to ninety meetings for their first ninety days of sobriety."

He is not impressed and is, in fact, getting annoyed at AA. He doesn't like that these strangers are telling me what to do. I wish I could repeat verbatim what Joy said to me. How she made it seem like it's the best for everyone, for our family. But when I tell Chris what she said, it sounds like she is making demands, like she is a drill sergeant. Still, Chris says okay and that he'll talk to the guys to see what they say. He says he has one more work email to send for the day. If I finish cleaning the kitchen, he'll send his email and then we can put the kids to bed and watch a show. We've been watching *Homeland* on Netflix.

"That sounds nice," I say. A familiar fear spikes when Chris goes to log on to the computer. There is nothing incriminating there anymore, no evidence of my affair. I know I haven't engaged in any nefarious activities, emailing people I shouldn't be emailing. And as far as I can tell, Chris isn't doing anything he shouldn't be doing either. Yet I still feel uncomfortable every time Chris gets on our home laptop.

The next day Chris calls from work to say the guys agreed to switch the studio night back to Thursday. It's better for them anyway. Only his brother gripes a little about the flip-flopping. Joy was right. It turns out not to be a big deal.

MUSHROOM CAPITAL OF THE WORLD

January 28–30, 2011
Twenty to twenty-two days sober

Our babysitter Bethany agrees to babysit for our next weekend away. It will be expensive, but we won't have to worry about feeling like we are taking advantage of my sister. Chris searches for something for us to do, a concert or show that we might like. He finds that Jim Boggia is playing at Kennett Flash, a small venue in Kennett Square, PA. Boggia has a song we both like that gets played on our local college radio station. The song reminisces about a couple driving around listening to the band NRBQ, just like Chris and I used to do when we were dating.

It's unspoken, but I can tell Chris is trying to reestablish connections between us. Bob and I talked about music, sharing favorite songs with each other. He compiled all the songs into a playlist on a thumb drive and gave it to me like a going-away present. After Chris learned of the affair, I threw away the thumb drive and tried to erase any evidence of the songs on the computer. But somehow Chris was able to find the playlist. It crushed him to learn that we had talked about music. Music is Chris's thing. He plays guitar and has a studio where he records songs with other musicians.

The computer became a source of anxiety for us. It held digital ghosts of texts, emails, and songs that were played the night I was with Bob. Chris couldn't handle the thought of using the computer that I had used to communicate with Bob. I hated the idea that he might accidentally stumble upon an exchange between me and Bob that I hadn't managed to erase. We agreed it was worthwhile to spend the money to get a new laptop. I'm not sure what Chris ever did with the old one. I'm sure that if we'd had a gun, he'd have taken it out to the backyard and shot it.

Chris plans the entire weekend away. We will stay in a bed-and-breakfast, go out to dinner, and then see Jim Boggia. The following day we'll visit Longwood Gardens, a horticultural park. In preparation for the weekend, I get a Brazilian bikini wax. I'm trying to do something different, show Chris I am making an effort too. The bikini wax does the trick, and on our drive down to Pennsylvania, we are both so turned on that Chris pulls the car into a train station parking lot and we have sex in the car in the middle of the day.

We check into our bed-and-breakfast. It feels weird, like we are in a guest room at someone's house, which I guess we are. We fling the pillows off the bed (it seems like there are hundreds), strip down, and climb into the soft, fluffy bed high off the floor. It feels so odd to be in bed in the middle of the day in this lacy Victorian room. We giggle like high school students and grope each other under the covers.

I bought a new outfit for tonight. "Skinny jeans" and a tight, sleeveless black shirt from Ann Taylor Loft. But when I get dressed I'm scared I'm going to be cold, so I put on a sweater over the sexy shirt.

At dinner, we learn Kennett Square is the mushroom capital of world. The waiter hands me the wine list and Chris immediately takes it from me. When we place our order, I feel like the waiter is disappointed that we don't order alcoholic drinks. No drinks means the bill is smaller, which means a smaller tip. I tell this to Chris and he says who cares what the waiter thinks. I order a dish with mushrooms even though that means I can't share with Chris because he doesn't like mushrooms. He says they taste like dirt. There are so many things Chris doesn't like that we end up not eating at home, like fish, tomatoes, and olives. I try to order those things when we go out to eat. But then Chris says I'm "defensive ordering," ordering a dish I know he won't eat so that I can't share. So I had stopped ordering things that I like in order to be able to share my dish with him. Tonight, I decide to order a dish with mushrooms because I like them. If I can't drink, I might as well enjoy my food. Plus, it is the mushroom capital of the world.

After dinner, we drive to the venue. It's a small theater where you sit at a table and a waitress brings you drinks. I scan the crowd. It's an eclectic mix of college students and middle-agers like us. A waitress goes by our table with a full tray of pints. The smell of wheat-y draft beer wafts past me. Chris gives me a smile and squeezes my hand. He is being supportive, but I can't help being resentful. He took a hit of weed from his bat when we parked the car. There's a two-year-old in my head that screams, "It's not fair."

Jim Boggia is awesome. He plays originals, including our song about NRBQ, and cool covers on his ukulele like "Thunder Road," which, me being a Jersey girl, is probably one of my top five songs. Then Boggia plays "Life on Mars," which was a song that I never liked. But this soft melodic version on the ukulele makes me cry.

Suddenly, I hit an invisible wall. It's so uncomfortable being sober in this club around all this drinking. I'm jittery and I feel my anger surge at Chris. I need to get out of there. I want to go back to the bed-and-breakfast and go to bed. I tell Chris I'm tired and luckily he agrees we should leave early.

The next day we walk around Longwood Gardens. It's cold but sunny. The property has these really cool tree houses, and we discuss bringing the kids back here.

It's time to head home. The car ride home is awkward. We scan songs on the radio but I'm terrified a song from Bob's playlist will pop on the radio. So instead I find the public radio station and I'm relieved when *Wait Wait . . . Don't Tell Me!* comes on. We are safe with a talk show.

Back at the house, we thank Bethany, handing her a big wad of cash. *Was it worth it*, I wonder? *Is our relationship fixed?* The kids drag me to the couch to watch a show with them. While I settle into our sectional with the kids snuggled by my side, Chris brings in our overnight bags and disappears to the basement to do the laundry.

A week later, my pubic hair starts to grow back from the Brazilian bikini wax and gets itchy. Instead of watching a show with me after dinner, Chris heads down to the basement. I hear the clunk of the washing machine kicking on. *What is he doing down there?* I worry.

HOME GROUP

Wednesday, February 2, 2011
Twenty-five days sober

On Wednesday night I depart my house at exactly 7:45 p.m. I know that it will only take me five minutes to drive to the church. That gives me five minutes to park and get to my seat. I pull into the long driveway that goes through the graveyard. My mom used to take us to this cemetery to do grave rubbings. It's dark and I'm worried I might hit the people walking towards my car as I drive down the driveway to a dirt parking lot. I squeeze into a parking spot and then follow the crowd up the paved driveway. I'm careful not to walk on any graves. Even though it's cold out, I'm starting to sweat. This meeting looks crowded. Not like the small Candlelight meeting I go to on Mondays or the Thursday night Women's Step meeting.

My panic rises when I walk in the back door of the parish house. The kitchen is crowded; people are bustling around making coffee and putting out cookies. This is the largest meeting I've been to yet. I feel a hand on my arm and turn to see Mary smiling at me. I almost hug her, I'm so relieved to see someone I know. Would I even call her a friend now?

"Come sit with us," she says and leads me to a four-person card table up front next to the podium. Alice sees me too and waves. Alice is another friendly face I've met in AA. She and Mary are often together. Coincidentally, we all sort of look the same, with blonde hair and glasses.

How come they are all here already? I thought I was early. Later I learn that people show up for home group an hour or more early to set up and make coffee. I feel out of sorts when I learn this. How come no one told me to come early?

Joy walks in after the meeting starts. I know that she can't leave for the meeting until her husband, who commutes into the city, comes home. She sits at a table with all men, who all seem to know her.

Now that I've been to a few meetings, I know that the script they read at the beginning of each meeting is specific to that particular meeting. At this one, the leader asks someone to read "How it Works," someone to read the "Ninth Step Promises," and someone to light the candle of hope. I feel left out that I haven't been asked to do any of these tasks. The leader asks the secretary to get up, and Mary leans over to me and says: "That's who you need to talk to after the meeting. You need to give him your name, number, and sober date." I nod but think, *Really, that guy?* He looks sketchy, with tattoos and ear piercings. Then the leader says, "Would all group members raise their hands?" Pretty much everyone in the place does. Then they all say, in unison, "Fine show of hands!" I laugh. What was that? I don't know but I like it. It reminds me of the call and response of an Irish Happy Hour I used to go to in college. I loved feeling part of a group and knowing the secret responses you are supposed to say at particular moments. I like this group. It has a fun energy.

Next the leader says, "Would any newcomers like to introduce themselves?" Joy gives me a look and I know what I'm supposed to do. I've learned this part. I raise my hand. "Hi. I'm

Liz. I have twenty-five days." Everyone claps. Alice and Mary smile at me. I shrug, smile back.

When the meeting is over, Mary and Alice ask me if I'm going to the diner. "Oh no," I say, thinking of Chris waiting at home for me.

"We go to the diner after every home group meeting," they explain. "You should come." "Okay, maybe next week," I say. I'm jealous of these two girls. They have no kids or husbands and appear to give all their free time to AA. I do not have that luxury.

When I get home, Chris is playing guitar in the study. He asks how it went.

"Good," I say. I explain about how large it is, how nice it was that Mary and Alice were there to greet me. I tell him about the "Fine show of hands" part. He doesn't respond. I get the sense he thinks I shouldn't be having so much fun at these meetings.

STARTING THE STEP WORK

> Step One: We admitted we were powerless over alcohol—that our lives had become unmanageable.

Thursday, February 3, 2011
Twenty-six days sober

Joy tells me that we'll meet once a week after the Thursday meeting at her house to do "step work." But first, I am to write my story—what it was like, what happened, and what it is like now—which I do, and I give it to her at our first Step Work meeting. She reads it while putting groceries away. *She is an amazing multitasker*, I think, but I'm a little annoyed that I'm not getting her full attention. Her response is, "Well, it looks like you are an alcoholic." I want more of a reaction. Isn't she shocked about the loss of my brother and sister? Doesn't she pity me? She says nothing about that. She tells me to open the Big Book, starting at the Foreword to the First Edition, and gives me an eye as if I'm going to challenge her on where we are to start reading from. She tells me, "First you read a paragraph out loud and then I will." We take turns reading, and I'm embarrassed when I stumble over unfamiliar words. When I balk a little about the awkwardness of the text, she explains that it was published in 1939. *Why don't they update it*, I think.

We read for about thirty minutes and then I'm dismissed. On my way out the door, she gives me my next assignment: make a T-chart. In one column, list how you are powerless over alcohol. Use specific examples. In the other column, list how your life is unmanageable. The two sides do not have to correlate.

I tell her I'm not going to have much in the unmanageable column. I mean, my life is pretty put together. I have a husband, a house, and three kids who I take care of. I have a part-time job and a bunch of friends. My life isn't unmanageable.

She tilts her head and looks at me when I explain all this.

"Okay, we'll see when you do the assignment. Bring it to our next meeting."

T-Chart

Powerless over alcohol	*How my life is unmanageable*
From the very first time in eighth grade, I drank until I threw up or passed out.	I would steal from the people I babysat for. Alcohol but sometimes money and clothes.
In high school, I was uncomfortable in social situations unless I was drinking.	I would steal money and goods from the video store I worked at.
Any opportunity to drink, I would.	I stole a ring from my sister Roseann and lied about it.
In high school, if there was nowhere to drink, I would throw a party even if my parents were just going out to dinner.	I would take things from my siblings without asking.
I would always have a drink BEFORE going out. At home while waiting to get picked up or in the car on the way to a bar or a friend's house.	I would lie to my parents to get out of trouble.
I would drink any type of alcohol that was available even if I hated the taste. I would often mix my mother's scotch with whatever juice was on hand.	I got picked up by the police for drinking with my friends at the river.

Powerless over alcohol	*How my life is unmanageable*
If there was alcohol in my home or apartment, I would drink it even if it wasn't mine.	I was brought into the police station twice for having parties at my parents' house.
When home by myself, I would often drink until I passed out.	On a trip to Cancún when I was seventeen years old, I left my friends at the bar and went off with some dude on a moped back to his hotel.
I could never drink just one drink. Given the opportunity, I would drink whatever alcohol was there until it was gone.	I took a blank check that my parents left for my sister Julia for her college tuition and used to get a keg for a party.
Even when I had events to go to, such as taking Ray to the doctor's, I would drink even though I only had to hold off drinking an hour or two.	I once drank my friend Kelly's champagne that was given to her and her fiancée as an engagement gift. I drank it and then replaced it and then drank the replacement bottle and replaced it again, etc. Finally, I realized my roommate didn't even notice and I stopped replacing it.
	I would hook up with guys who I didn't even like.
	In college, I crashed my dad's Volvo into a median on the highway. I have no idea where I was going. I don't even remember leaving the bar. I vowed to quit drinking but that lasted maybe three days.
	On my twenty-first birthday, I drank so much that I passed out in an alleyway outside the bar by nine o'clock.
	I would drink to fall asleep and then drink coffee to wake up again and again.
	In high school, I got stitches in my head after bumping it but I still went to a party that night and drank.
	Once I went flying off a trampoline and fell on my face, but I still went to a party that night and drank.

Powerless over alcohol	*How my life is unmanageable*
	One December in my twenties, I was drinking at a bar with a friend. We went to leave and I slipped on the ice and fell on my face. My hands were in my pockets and I had nothing to protect my face when it hit the curb. I still went home with the guy and drank some more and hooked up.
	I've missed school or work due to hangovers.
	Most times when I drank, I would throw up, either that night or the next day. One time, while hungover babysitting, I threw up in Rumson Country Club's parking lot.
	One time I showed up to babysit high. I think the mother knew.
	I drove drunk by myself and with other people in the car and, when I became a mom, with my kids in the car.
	I was given a paid leave by the newspaper where I worked and then on the day I was supposed to return I just didn't show up.
	In my twenties, I was offered a job and then on my first day I didn't show up or call to tell them I didn't want the job.
	I would often lose my keys, license, passport, a folder called "important documents," etc.
	I would hide empty bottles of beer from Chris so that he wouldn't see how much I drank.
	When Julia was still nursing, I drank.
	Sometimes I would leave the kids home alone while they were asleep to run to the liquor store.
	I accidentally put Michael's Halloween costume in Ray's backpack. Michael had to borrow one from the school for his parade.

Powerless over alcohol	*How my life is unmanageable*
	Once I drank before taking Ray to his doctor's appointment and was nonchalant about Ray's asthma, telling the doctor with a shrug, "He is always wheezing."
	I've been drunk when I picked up the kids from preschool.
	I opened a credit card to hide purchases from Chris, including alcohol. In order to pay off the credit card, I had to get money orders from the post office because I couldn't just write a check. So I had to get cash from the grocery store, but more often than not I would use that cash to buy alcohol.
	I once passed out while the boys were watching a TV show. Michael was two and a half and Ray was about six months. I woke up and found Michael squeezing ketchup into a bowl. I threw up into the kitchen garbage and when Chris came home and said it smelled like puke, I blamed it on the kids.
	I did not perform to the best of my ability at work. I once didn't get around to mailing a whole packet of marketing letters my dad had written and I threw them out instead of admitting to my dad that I never mailed them.
	Sometimes I would drink while working.
	I showed up drunk to a joint therapy appointment with my sister. We were there to work out some problems we had been having.
	I would suffer from horrible bouts of depression. I would see a therapist but never tell the therapist how much I drank. In fact, I would lie about it. Why pay for a therapist and then lie to them?
	In my twenties, I would spend hours drinking and smoking cigarettes while staring into the bathroom mirror and listening to music and crying.
	I had an affair.

THE DINER

February 9 and 16, 2011
Thirty-two and Thirty-nine days sober

"We all go to the diner after the meeting," says Joy. This is said as an invitation, but I know it's not. It's not even a suggestion—it's a command. *If you want what we have, do what we do.* And I do want what they have. Alice, Mary, and Joy: beautiful, smart women, well put together in cute outfits. Before the meetings they run around the room moving furniture and setting up a rack with brochures, all the while happily chitchatting with everyone. They are so self-assured, while I sit there feeling grubby in jeans and a T-shirt. Too nervous to go get a cup of coffee from the kitchen, I rummage through my purse looking for my phone. I aimlessly check messages and then flip the switch on the side to turn the ringer off. I'm acutely aware that everyone else is in conversation and I have no one to talk to. I don't actually want to talk to anyone, but at the same time I'm annoyed that no one is talking to me. Don't they know I'm new? Shouldn't they be asking how I'm doing? Don't they know that my marriage is falling apart? It will take years before I realize it's not all about me. In fact, I'm still working on it.

Mary and Alice are my "sober sisters," which means we share the same sponsor, Joy. Up until two weeks ago, I couldn't tell them apart. They are both pretty, have long, straight blond hair, wear glasses, and come and talk to me. They know so much about AA. I feel like an idiot around them. They are in the club, and I don't yet know the secret handshake.

When they ask me how I'm doing, I try to explain. Explain about what it's like in my house. The suffocating air, the tension, how anger pulsates off my husband Chris, making it unbearable to be in the same room with him. They respond by asking what step I'm on. It's off-putting. I want someone to listen to me and agree with me. Sure, I am a cheating, lying alcoholic, but he has hurt me for years. In my opinion, this mess we are in is all his fault. But no one seems to care about my opinion, except for my therapist. When I talk about Chris's faults to these AA folks, they cut me off and ask me what meetings I'm going to. Then they suggest other ones.

I tell my sponsor that I can't go to the diner. I told Chris I'd be home after the meeting.

"Yes, if we say we are going to be home at a certain time, then that's what we do," she nods. The message comes through loud and clear. My days of lying and manipulating are over. I do what I say, and I say what I do.

"Tell Chris that we all go to the diner after the meeting, so that next week you can come," she says brightly. She swings her purse on her shoulder, indicating our conversation is over.

"Call me tomorrow!" she says with a smile and turns away to talk to someone else. I'm dismissed.

I'm nervous to tell Chris about the diner. He won't like the idea of me socializing with strangers and strange men. And I can't blame him. He has a right to be distrustful. I tell Joy about my fears on the phone the next day.

"Well, we can't be afraid to ask," is her response. But I am afraid. Things have just started to get better. In fact, last night we both got a good night's sleep, something that hasn't happened in a while. Every night since December Chris wakes up in the middle of the night, around three or four in the morning. I can feel him awake and that wakes me up. I remain still and pretend that I'm asleep so as not to disturb him. I pray that he goes back to sleep. But often we just lie like that, awake in bed not moving, until it's time to get up and grab that first cup of coffee. Then, last night, he slept through the night, so that means I did too. I didn't wake up until three-year-old Julia crawled into bed next to me at five o'clock.

The next day, after our first cup of coffee, I tell Chris about going to the diner after the meeting on Wednesday nights. I tell him, despite not wanting to piss him off and despite not wanting to go at all, because deep down somewhere in my unconscious, I know that my life depends on this. I know that going to the diner after the meeting is the difference between stopping drinking and staying stopped. No one has told me this, but I just know. *If you want what we have, do what we do.*

"Joy is insisting I go," I tell Chris, trying to hide the nervous tic in my voice that might suggest I'm hiding something. He puts down his coffee and turns to the kitchen sink to wash a pot that has been soaking in the sink overnight. He's annoyed. I imagine he's thinking, *Who is this woman who can tell you what to do?*

If Chris only knew how badly I wanted to drink. How badly I wanted to say fuck this, fuck AA, and fuck you all, and to grab a handle of vodka and lock myself in the closet. If he knew that I would forsake everything—our marriage, our house, and our kids—for that closet and that bottle of vodka, he'd give me some more slack. He's trying to learn. He's going to Al-Anon.

All week I stress about going to the diner. I've never been a fan of eating at diners. Chris, on the other hand, a real New Yorker, loves diners. In his twenties, he and his friends would end their nights at the Main Street Diner in Huntington, Long Island. I can picture them, a ragtag group of musicians and artists, smoking, harassing the waitress, sobering up with a cheeseburger and a cup of coffee. My nights never ended like that. They ended with me passed out in puke somewhere. There was no post-bar event for me. I never made it that long. Or if I did, I certainly didn't remember it. When we were dating, Chris would suggest the diner as an option for dinner, but I never wanted to go. I wouldn't have been able to explain why at the time. But years later, the reason was revealed to me by a man speaking from the podium at a meeting. He said: "I never went to the diner when I was drinking because diners don't serve alcohol." Oh, yeah, that's why! Instead of the diner, I would suggest a chain restaurant like TGI Fridays or Chili's, with their laminated drink menus: pages and pages of yummy-sounding "hand-crafted cocktails" like Tropical Berry Mojito Shaker or Pink Punk Martini. I'm not sure who I was fooling, ordering those fancy drinks. Just give me a tumbler full of vodka and splash some lemonade or cranberry juice on top and I'd be fine.

But now I have thirty-two (or is it thirty-three?) days sober and I'm expected to go to the diner with a bunch of strangers after an AA meeting. When the meeting is over, I ask Alice and Mary if they're going. There is no way I'm going unless one of them is going. I need someone there who I have had at least one or two conversations with already. They confirm they are, thank God. I double-check that the diner where everyone goes is the one down the street from the meeting. I have a vague recollection of where it is, but I've never been there, even though it's around the corner from my house. The day before the meeting, I made sure I had cash and then I broke the $20 so that I have ones and fives. I don't want to be at the diner and have to figure out how to split a bill with only a $20 bill.

Alice and Mary are lingering after the meeting. I want to walk out with them, to make sure we arrive at the diner at the same time, but I'm tired of waiting around. I'm getting anxious. I decide to just bite the bullet and go. Plus, I don't see Joy anywhere. She might already be there. To get to the diner, I must make a difficult left-hand turn out of the church parking lot, crossing two lanes of traffic. The click of the car's turn signal seems extra loud as I wait for a chance to pull out. I could turn right and head home. Chris will have just put the kids to bed. We could watch an *Arrested Development* episode together on the couch. But just as I have that thought, the traffic clears and it's my chance to make a left-hand turn. So I do.

The diner is your classic Greek, all-American establishment. In fact, it's called "The Americana Diner." The outside looks like a '50s throwback, with red and silver paneling. It's got a big neon sign with the Statue of Liberty's torch as the *i* in "American." I park and walk towards the door with purpose. Several people I recognize from the meeting are outside smoking. *Here we go*, I think. When I enter the lobby I note the typical diner smell, coffee and pancakes, even though it's after nine o'clock. I stand awkwardly looking at the host, not sure what to do or say (*do I say I'm here with AA?*), when Alice walks in and smiles at me.

"We have a table in the back," she tells me and leads me past the host and the booths to the back of the diner. I am stunned at the scene. The wait staff has set up a long table, enough spots for at least twenty, and it is already almost full.

Alice sits down in the middle of the table, and I take a seat across from her, squeezing behind the row of chairs. I'm more comfortable with my back against the wall, facing out. I don't like people sneaking up behind me.

I order my standard diner fare: a grilled cheese, American cheese on whole wheat bread. I am shocked at how well the waitress is handling this crowd. *How are we going to split the check?* I wonder. It's going to be a nightmare. At the end of the night, I discover that the waitress gives everybody their own check, even if it's only for a cup of coffee.

Soon after we place our orders, the waitress, whose name I've learned is Karen, plops down five small dishes of coleslaw and pickles.

"I threw some extra pickles in there," she tells us.

"Thank you, Karen," the table says in sing-song unison. The small dishes are immediately claimed. I never knew people actually ate the coleslaw at diners. Wasn't there a thing about how they recycle the coleslaw, so you shouldn't eat it? These people have never heard that theory. They are devouring the coleslaw. The woman next to me starts to pout, complaining that someone took her coleslaw. She glares around at the other diners, who are ignoring her. I got a sandwich so I guess I should have been given a coleslaw too, but I don't say anything about my missing coleslaw.

I chat awkwardly with the woman next to me, whose name is either Deanna or Diana. She tells me her story. It's easy enough to sit there and listen. Joy breezes into the back room about an hour later. She squeezes in next to Mary and Alice and begins to pick at their french fries. When the waitress asks her if she wants anything she says no. In fact, I've never seen Joy order anything from the diner, ever. She just comes, socializes, eats any leftover cake, and goes.

I look around the table and see Alice and Mary. There's Marie, a loud, black-haired Italian woman who later earns the nickname "Guidos and Booze" because she ends her story with, "Now I know there is more to life than guidos and booze." There's the loveable Josh, the handsome gay artist. His laugh reminds me of Eddie Murphy. And just like Eddie, when Josh laughs you can't help but laugh along.

The conversation flows easily enough. A burst of laughter explodes at the other end of the table. I tell my table neighbors, "We can't let it seem like they are having more fun. Let's laugh really hard." And I let out a hearty guffaw, which gets everyone around me to laugh. We get looks from the other end of the table, which makes us laugh harder. I'm coming out of my shell. People are starting to realize there is more to me than the pouty girl in the ponytail.

Karen passes out the checks. I'm amazed at this level of order management. She deserves a huge tip as far as I'm concerned. People throw dollars in the middle of the table. I throw a couple into the pile. I scoot out of my seat and wave goodbye to everyone. I go to the front desk to pay. That was another thing that I disliked about diners: bringing your check up to pay. But now I'm grateful, because I don't want to make a long exit. I just want to wave goodbye and get out of there.

When I push open the doors and step out onto the stoop, I'm hit with a fresh February breeze. I survived my first night of the diner and I even had a little fun. It was nice to learn more about the people at the meeting. Our home group is a speaker meeting, which means people from other home groups come and speak to our group. Because of that format, we never get to hear the stories of our fellow home groupers. Tonight, at the diner, I heard Diana's (Deena's?) story. I listened and she appreciated it. For a little while I was thinking about someone else instead of my own problems.

When I walk into the house, Chris is playing guitar in the study. He has a look on his face. It's the "I'm worried but I'm not going to show it" look. Does he know how easy it is to read his emotions? I tell him about the diner. I explain it was awkward but also nice. I tell him about how we fake laughed. Then I say, "Let's watch *Arrested Development*," and his look disappears. He hangs up his guitar and joins me on the couch.

LUDLOW

Step Two: Came to believe that a Power greater than ourselves could restore us to sanity.

March 4–6, 2011
Fifty-five to fifty-eight days sober

It's a Thursday night in March and Chris, the kids, and I are packed into the minivan on our way to Ludlow, Vermont. We are headed for a long weekend away at Kelly's parents' vacation house, a comfortable ski lodge that sits on a hill above the town of Ludlow, overlooking Okemo Mountain. Kelly and I and my other college friend MaryBeth have been gathering at this house once a year since we graduated college in 1995. I see Kelly more often, being that we both live in New Jersey. MaryBeth lives in Vermont, about two hours north of Ludlow, and I only get to see her once a year, on this weekend.

First we came as single women in our twenties, although Kelly and Scott were together even back then. Then we married and brought our spouses. And then, every year, one or two babies would join the group. Michael was the first baby to arrive and Julia was the last. In between them, there's Kelly's Mary and Will and MaryBeth's two girls, Madeline and Rose. Miraculously, all three husbands and seven kids get along exceptionally well.

The car ride is taking longer than it should because Chris insisted we stop for a sit-down dinner in New Paltz, NY. My preference is to avoid long stops. I suggested we hit a McDonald's drive-thru to keep making time. But for some reason, Chris likes to stop in this college town and eat at this one restaurant, the Main Street Bistro. And although I won't admit it, his call was the right one. The food was fresh and the kids enjoyed stretching their legs as we walked up and down Main Street for a little bit. It was much more pleasant than shoveling down hamburgers and fries in the stuffy minivan.

After dinner, we continue north on the New York Thruway. It's unusually quiet in the back and I turn around to see that both Julia and Raymond have fallen asleep. Julia, who has just turned three, is still in a car seat and gets the luxury of a headrest, into which she presses her little face. Raymond, five, gets to sit in a big boy booster seat. But it doesn't have a back, so his head flops uncomfortably over to the side. Occasionally he wakes up and repositions himself while clutching his yellow blankie. Sleeping now may mean they will stay up later tonight, but it makes for an easier trip, so I'm relieved. Michael sits on the bench seat in the way back. The glow from his iPad lights up his pale face and he seems small and vulnerable. I wish there was a way I could move his seat closer to me. But he likes it back there, away from his parents.

We exit the New York State Thruway, when Chris starts in on me. "You know, he might be there, skiing with his family."

"What are you talking about?" I ask, although I know what he is getting at.

"Your dude," he says. "He might be skiing at Okemo this weekend. We could run into him."

"He is not my 'dude,' and I wouldn't know his plans because I haven't been in touch with him since October," I say.

"I hope that's true," Chris says, taking his eyes off the road to stare me down with a familiar glare, a glare that projects accusation and superiority and condemnation through his large brown eyes. Day after day I get this look, and I hate it. Now I want to throw my to-go coffee in his face and burn the glare away. Chris is right though. I had thought of it too. Bob's family are skiers. It's possible that he too is on his way to go skiing at this family-friendly resort with his wife and three kids. But to Chris I insist that it's a ludicrous notion. Then I do what I always do: turn the accusations on him.

"What about you?" I say through clenched teeth. "How do I know you haven't been in touch with Kathy or Robin?" *You have done things too!* I scream at him in my head.

"I haven't been," he says. "Go ahead and look through my email or the phone records."

"Yeah, well, I haven't been in touch with anyone I shouldn't be talking to either."

Chris doesn't respond but stares ahead and grips the steering wheel tightly. Now I'm getting the silent treatment. *Fine.* I clam up too and stare out the window. We ride along the cold Hudson River in Albany and pass by the ugly chain stores and restaurants of Troy. I quietly seethe inside, thinking about how he doesn't get it. He doesn't realize how hard this weekend will be for me. How everyone will be drinking beer. Probably my favorite beer, Magic Hat #9. How I have never been away for a ski weekend without drinking. All he cares about is what I did. Does he even care if I stay sober?

Although it is dark out, I can feel the landscape change as we cross the border from New York into Vermont. Now off the big highway and its ugly billboards, we are on winding, hilly Route 11. We pass Bromley Mountain. There is nothing much alongside the road but patches of white snow and tall evergreen trees. As we drive up a long, steep incline, the headlights shine on a wispy fog. Inside the car, the heavy air of accusations begins to lift. The atmosphere is lighter.

"Is this Terrible Mountain?" I ask, knowing Chris will roll his eyes at this. Kelly always insists that this route goes over Terrible Mountain, but Chris scoffs at the notion that it's a terrible mountain. To him, it's just a hill.

"If it is, it's nothing that I and this ole girl can't handle." He pats the plastic console of the minivan and mutters, "Good girl," as if it was the neck of a horse pulling us across the wild frontier. I smile at him and the mood lightens some more. We are okay now. This is how it goes: we fight and then we recover, fight and recover.

We arrive at the ski house a little after nine o'clock. Kelly, Scott, and their kids, Mary and Will, are all still up and they greet us enthusiastically. When we've lugged all our bags and food into the house, we sit with our friends by the fire. Chris's mood darkens again. He is embarrassed in front of his friend Scott. Realizing that Scott and Kelly know part of the story, he feels like less of a man. When we go to bed in the guest room in the basement, Chris is angry and hurt again and I'm defensive and angry back. Here we go again.

The next morning, Chris takes off early for the first ski run of the day. Okemo lets you take one free run to see if you want to commit to a full day of skiing. Chris takes advantage of this to hit the slope without paying the exorbitant ticket price. I don't think the rest of us will ski this year. Although the Northeast was dumped with a blizzard at the end of December, since then the weather has warmed. In fact, last month, the kids and I were frolicking on the beach and Raymond even went in the ocean. It is cold here in Vermont and the ski resort makes snow, but still, the conditions aren't great and we don't have the energy to ski anyway. It takes all our energy just to make it through the day.

MaryBeth and her family aren't arriving until dinnertime. Kelly says when Chris comes back from skiing we should go to the local coffee shop, Java Babba's, and then hit the supermarket on the way home.

When we walk into the coffee shop, a man dressed in a tie-dye shirt with long gray hair pulled back into a ponytail holds the door open for us and says, "Peace and love." I smile and think, only in Vermont. I am more comfortable in this state. I look like everyone else here, in my Merrell hiking shoes and jeans. When I wear the same thing at school pickup in New Jersey, I feel underdressed.

I order a dark roast and Kelly gets a chai latte.

"Not as good as Starbuck's," she says with a sigh. We start talking. She wants to know the full story. Not the stuff about the affair. She wants to know about the stuff I really hid. The drinking at home with the kids during the day. I tell her bits and pieces. How I would drink and drive the kids around. How, when Chris was out of town, I would drink until I passed out, sometimes on the floor of the kids' bedroom. How I even left the kids home alone sometimes to go buy a bottle from the liquor store. I tell her all of this matter-of-factly, without emotion. I don't feel one way or another about it. It is the facts. But my disclosures are upsetting Kelly and she starts to cry. She wipes the tears off her cheeks with the sleeve of her sweatshirt. I'm surprised by her tears. Why is this so sad? Not until a year later do I realize she is not crying for me but for my kids. She is upset about how close I came to something seriously bad happening. A marriage falling apart is one thing, but she realizes I could have killed my children. AA calls these things that could've happened the "Not yets." I've stopped drinking before something truly bad happened, but it could still happen, if I started drinking again. But at this point, two months sober, I'm not scared about the Not yets. That I drove around drunk with my kids in the car doesn't upset me the way it's upsetting Kelly. At this time, what upsets me, what terrifies me, what causes my stomach to flip and my hands to shake, is that I can no longer drink.

When we get back to the house, the kids are in the living room while Scott preps for dinner. The Buntings still haven't arrived. I head down to the bottom floor, where our guest bedroom is. The door to the bedroom is closed. I open it without knocking and walk in. Chris is kneeling on the floor next to the bed, his hands folded together and his head bent so that it touches the bed's blue patchwork quilt. I quickly back out of the room and close the door. He's praying for God's sake. Is he doing this to show me how much he is hurting inside? I get it, Chris, I hurt you! Enough with this show.

Finally, MaryBeth and her family arrive, and we all sit down to eat a chicken dinner. I note that Scott and Kelly aren't drinking at dinner. Kelly rarely drinks so I'm not surprised by that, but Scott normally has a beer with dinner. I know he enjoys microbrews and even makes his own beer in his garage. I'm annoyed that he isn't having one now. *Please don't make this awkward. Everyone should just drink if they want to drink. Just because I can't doesn't mean you shouldn't.* Then I notice MaryBeth's large glass of white wine and that her husband Adam is on his second or maybe third beer, and I get annoyed. *You know I can't drink; can't you forgo a drink for one fucking dinner?* I know what my sponsor, Joy, would say: this just proves that you are an alcoholic. Normally people don't obsess about what other people are drinking.

Later, as we are getting ready for bed in our guest bedroom, Chris acknowledges how hard this weekend must be for me. To not drink. And I say yes, but I'll be okay. I tell him that Joy told me I should try to go to a meeting while I'm here. I looked up the meetings earlier in the week and there is one in town tomorrow night; I ask him if I can go.

"Sure," he says. "Whatever you gotta do." But I feel like he doesn't want me to go. We are on vacation and I still have to go to meetings. My disease is an inconvenience.

While lying in bed, I think about what it was like last year on this trip. I remember that the Sierra Nevadas I was openly drinking were not getting the job done. I wasn't buzzed enough. So, when the men went out to the store to pick up steaks and MaryBeth and Kelly were upstairs changing, I opened and closed the cupboards in the kitchen and dining areas, searching the ski house for its liquor cabinet. I found it and was relieved to see a bottle of vodka. Not my usual brand, but I didn't care. I grabbed a drinking glass and looked over my shoulder to make sure the kids were watching TV. Without picking up the bottle from the shelf, I screwed open the top and tilted the vodka into my glass. Then, topping it off with some orange juice from the fridge, I slugged it back and felt the immediate cascade of calm smoothing out my edges. I rinsed the glass carefully to remove the alcohol fumes and took a swig of my beer. I did that two more times that night. Now, lying in bed, my face flushes with shame at the memory and I snuggle up to Chris to push the thoughts away. To my relief, he wraps his arms around me, and I am comforted.

The next day, Saturday, the men decide to go snowshoeing on whatever snow there is in the woods. They just want out of the house and away from the kids. Chris wants away from me and the pain I've caused him. I wish I could wave a magic wand and make everything better. I've stopped drinking but everything is still so fucked up.

With the husbands gone and the kids in the basement watching a movie, Kelly, MaryBeth, and I sit in the living room next to the fire. Large windows look out onto Okemo Mountain. MaryBeth and Kelly are sharing a knit blanket, snuggled next to each other on the green couch, drinking tea. They are talking about what's new in their jobs. They are both the main breadwinners of their families and have professional, high-powered positions in their companies. When they talk like this, I feel like a stupid housewife. Sure, I have my personal assistant job, but booking my boss's/dad's travel and organizing his files is not on the same level as their RFPs and business meetings.

While they chat, I grab the binoculars that hang next to the large glass doors and strain to see people skiing down the mountain. Little dots move across a white space. *Look at all those people who are just living life. Normal people out skiing with their families. They are not loser alcoholics like me.* I hang the binoculars back on their hook and stare out at the whole countryside. The sky is gray but it's too warm out for snow. Too bad, because this bleak world could use a nice blanket of fresh white snow. In the distance, a black freight train moves slowly across the frozen fields.

The talk in the living room shifts from professional life to more personal matters. Kelly asks me about my sponsor. What is she like? I sit down on the glider across from the couch.

"I probably wouldn't be friends with Joy in real life," I say. "She's too . . ." I struggle to explain. "Intense, maybe. I don't know. She exercises a lot. But she's a great sponsor. She always seems to know the right thing to say." I explain to them that Joy is currently taking me through the Twelve Steps. I'm on Step Two.

"I need to turn my will over to a higher power of my understanding," I try to explain. Kelly and MaryBeth are intrigued, so I go on. I say that I'm stuck on the idea that I have no will. That everything I do is part of God's plan. I just can't wrap my head around that. And Kelly and MaryBeth agree. We discuss what this means. Is God involved in every decision we make? It's nice to talk with them openly about this. It reminds me of the discussions we had back in college, sitting around our dorm room, playing Mancala. Last year I needed vodka to sit and talk with them. This year I'm doing it sober, and it feels good. I feel connected. I ask them if they want to come to the meeting with me tonight. They say yes. Back then, I wanted everyone to be a part of AA. Nowadays, I would never ask a nonalcoholic to attend a meeting with me. But when I first got sober, I wanted everyone to see what I was doing.

Later in the afternoon, we agree to have pizza for dinner so that Scott doesn't have to cook again. We can pick it up on our way home from the meeting. The husbands don't mention anything about the meeting, but Kelly and MaryBeth must have told them that's where we are going. There is an awkwardness in the air as we get our coats and shoes on, but we just plow forward. That's what I do these days: plunge ahead through the weirdness and discomfort.

When the meeting begins, I realize that the meeting I randomly picked is a Step meeting and the group is currently on Step Two. How crazy is that? I'm struggling with Step Two and I end up at a meeting in Vermont that's discussing Step Two! A woman shares how she is having trouble with the whole God thing. She says it really bothers her that the "Our Father" is said at the end of meetings. Instead of reciting it, she says the "Serenity Prayer" in her head. I used to feel that way too, but somehow I've learned to accept it. I see her point, but in my head I think, *Get over it.* I raise my hand and share. In a shaky voice, I say I'm new, only two months sober. I too am struggling with my concept of a higher power and have trouble understanding how to give up my will. I end with saying I'm grateful to have good friends to talk to, as I smile at MaryBeth and Kelly. The meeting ends with the "Our Father," and I look over at the woman who shared and see her lips move to "to accept the things I cannot change . . ."

We get in the car and drive to Wicked Good Pizza to pick up dinner. Kelly laughs that she wishes she were an alcoholic. She wants to go through the Twelve Steps.

"It would help everyone," I agree. MaryBeth is mostly quiet. I'm a little embarrassed about the meeting. Maybe she thinks it's all a bunch of cultish, New Age-y crap. I feel that way at times. But I keep going because I don't know what else to do.

When we arrive back at the ski house, the men are having their turn in the living room, talking next to the fire. Chris is sitting on the brick hearth, plucking on his guitar. I smile at him and he smiles back. Outside the large glass windows, snowflakes begin to fall.

FINDING MY HIGHER POWER

Step Three: Made a decision to turn our will and our lives over to the care of God as we understood Him.

April 2011
Three months sober

On the way home from dropping the kids off at school on Monday, I realize I didn't call Joy yesterday or the day before. The whole weekend went by and I did not pick up the phone. I'm supposed to call her every day. Although most of the time, when I call, she doesn't pick up. I leave a voicemail but she never calls back unless I say specifically, "I have a problem. Please call me back." It annoys me that she never returns my calls. I've discussed it with Alice.

"Oh yeah, Joy will never, ever call you. You always have to call her," Alice explained with a shrug. I could tell that she thinks it's odd too, but she's accepted it as the way it is with Joy. We sponsees are expected to call our sponsor every day, not only to check in but also to show our willingness to do something we don't want to do.

At first, my desperation made me willing to do anything. But as things have started to get better, I've started to balk at some of the "suggestions," aka requirements. And that is why, on days when I don't have a problem, I don't feel like calling Joy. Or sometimes I just forget. And calling your sponsor is like running; if you skip a day, it's that much harder to motivate to do it the following day. If you skip three days, it's really difficult to pick up the phone. It's so much easier to call when I have a problem—a fight with Chris or an incident at the kids' school. I explain the situation, she gives me a suggestion, I agree with her usually (in theory at least), and we hang up. Conversations in which I don't have anything to complain about are awkward. We don't have an easy rapport, Joy and me. It's not Joy's fault. I'm bad on the phone in general. One time Bob and I planned a phone date on a day that Chris and the kids went to visit his family in Long Island, and our conversation was so stifled. We paused awkwardly and stumbled over things to talk about. I hung up thinking, I *don't know if we really have the chemistry I thought we did.* If only I'd called the whole thing off then and there. But instead, I downed several vodka drinks and called him back an hour later. The second call went much more smoothly; we flirted casually like we did in our email correspondences. Too bad liquid confidence is no longer an option for me. Add that to the list of things that are difficult to get through now that I can't drink: parties, weddings, funerals, and phone conversations.

I've gotten yelled at before for not checking in. No, not yelled at. That's not right. Joy never yells. Scolds maybe, but not even that. She never makes you feel ashamed for digressions such as missing a meeting, leaving early, or not calling. She makes her point by telling her story or maybe even the story of another sponsee. She makes it clear through examples that in order to stay sober you have to do these things. And I want to stay sober and be a good sponsee, I do. So when I come home from dropping the kids off, I make a fresh pot of coffee and call her on my cell phone as I put the breakfast dishes in the dishwasher. She surprises me today by answering on the second ring. When it's clear I don't have any dilemma to discuss this morning, she asks, "Where are you in your step work?" I report that I've done everything she has asked me to do up to this point.

Two weeks ago, I wrote out my God-conscious moments, as Joy instructed: times in my life when I felt that my higher power was watching out for me. I thought I'd only be able to think of a couple of moments. My initial feeling was that God hasn't been present in my life. That's why my life is so screwed up. But as I started writing, I thought of more and more instances: The dozens (who I am kidding, hundreds) of times I'd gotten behind the wheel drunk and didn't die or, worse, kill someone else. The times in my teens and twenties when I'd put myself in dangerous situations and make it out okay. Even that moment on the deck when I revealed to Chris that I'd been drinking could be attributed to my higher power. It certainly wasn't my doing. I didn't want to tell Chris about my drinking because then I knew I would have to stop. Some other power pulled the words out of my mouth.

After I finished writing out all my God-conscious moments and shared the list with Joy, she told me to circle in red pen all the references in the Big Book to some type of higher power. This was an easy task, but I was annoyed that I had to go back through the Big Book again. First, Joy told me to read it on my own, which I did. Next, I had to meet with Joy to read it together, each of us taking turns reading paragraphs out loud. Then, I had to go through the book and circle all the references to how alcohol affects your mind and body. Finally, I had to go back through it again to find references to God. I may have let out an exasperated sigh when she gave me that task, but as usual, I did as I was told. There are some interesting higher power references in there: "Spirit of the Universe," "All Powerful, Guiding, Creative Intelligence," and "Infinite Power and Love." And as I completed my assignment, I got the point. AA wants you to pick your own version of God. They offer all sorts of descriptions so you can find one that suits you. I've heard in meetings some people say that their higher power is the people of AA. Others call it "Good Orderly Direction" or Mother Nature. Some people describe their God as on old man with a long white beard. *Really*? I think.

With the phone cradled on my shoulder, I bag up the kitchen trash and take it outside to dump it in the garbage can. I note that the daffodils I planted last October along our wooden fence are in bloom. Last fall seems so long ago. Last fall I'd be coming out to the garbage bins to hide empty vodka bottles underneath the household garbage. I don't want to go back to that tortuous time when I couldn't stop drinking, when I broke my marriage vows, when I was a shell of a person. The yellow and white teacup heads of the daffodils bopping in the breeze tell me I don't have to. I can move forward.

To Joy I say, "I was waiting for you to tell me what to do next." That's a fib. We both know I could have told her when I was finished circling references to a higher power and actively asked her what was next. Instead I passively waited for her to tell me the next step.

"Okay," she says enthusiastically. "Where do you want to do your Third Step?"

"What do you mean?"

"Some people like to go to the beach, or the woods, or somewhere special." She pauses when I don't immediately respond. "Or we can just meet at my house . . ."

"Your house is fine." I cut her off from listing more options. I can barely squeeze in the time to drive the five minutes to her house and sit for an hour. I can't imagine turning our get-togethers into a whole outing at the beach. Plus, I'm still uncomfortable around Joy. The thought of being in the car, driving to a destination . . . no thanks.

"Your house is fine," I repeat. We pick a date and time: next Monday after school drop-off. She gives me my instructions: "Write out a description of your concept of a higher power."

As with my other step work, I don't complete this task right away. I figure I have a week, so what's the rush. That night I go to the Monday night beginners' meeting. I'm the leader now, which I both like and dislike. I'm glad that I'm doing something for AA. "Being of service," as they say. It does make me feel useful to pass on what was "freely given to me." But I get nervous sitting at the head of the table, speaking in front of a group, and calling on people to share. I'm not good with remembering people's names and I panic when I call on people. Sometimes my voice shakes and then I get embarrassed, so it shakes more. I feel like an idiot when that happens. But my friends who are in the meeting say I'm doing great, so I keep showing up anyway.

Wednesday comes, and I go to Home Group. Afterwards, Joy asks if I've done my description yet.

"Not yet," I say with a smile. "Tomorrow for sure!"

"Okay," she says with a laugh. She knows I'm procrastinating.

I don't do my step work on Thursday, but Friday comes and I feel like I have some extra free time. Chris is at work, the kids are at school, and my boss/father is out of town on business so I don't have to work. I can sit and really think about this. After dropping the kids off at school, I brew a fresh pot of coffee, find an empty notebook and a pen, and sit down at the kitchen table. I think it's going to be hard but it actually flows out of me pretty easily:

I was raised Roman Catholic and have received all my sacraments, although I never connected with the Catholic version of God. I believe Jesus was a real person but not that he was born through Immaculate Conception. However, when I do attend church, I do feel connected to a higher power through prayer and the music. I especially love when there is a choir with instruments. When the choir sings "Joy to the World" with trumpets at Christmas Eve mass I'm moved to tears.

I went to a Catholic college where it was a requirement to take two religion courses. I found that I enjoyed learning about religions and the bible, specifically the Old Testament. I ended up being a Religious Studies major. It was philosophy, literature, and history all rolled up into one. I can see that even back then I was seeking some sort of spirituality.

I often feel connected to a higher power when in nature, and that is something my mother instilled in me: God is in the trees, in the deer in the fields, in the babbling brook. But even though I make it a priority to surround myself with nature, that isn't enough to fill my spiritual hole.

My version of a higher power is unexplainable, undefinable, cannot be pictured in a physical form; it is not any sort of being. It doesn't live in heaven or on a cross. "Spirit of the Universe" might be the closest thing to describe it. I've had many moments when I've felt this spirit course through. Music often connects me to my higher power. I had one particular moment when I was in Vermont with my family and friends: the song "Hey, Soul Sister," by Train, came on the radio and all the kids started dancing and singing to it. I was washing dishes and Kelly pulled me away from the sink and got me to dance. It was a

> collective moment of happiness, and I was overwhelmed with love and gratitude. I felt my higher power in that moment telling me it was going to be all right.

When I'm done, I close my notebook with satisfaction. I'm hungry and make myself a peanut butter sandwich. I look forward to meeting with Joy on Monday morning.

On Monday, I drive to Joy's house. It is drizzling and there's a bit of a chill in the air for April. Instead of our usual spot in her kitchen, she directs us to her living room. She asks me to read my description and she nods through it. She doesn't need to comment. She just needs to know that I have a sense of who my higher power is.

"There is one thing, though," I say.

"What?" she asks.

"I can't believe that it was God's will to have my sister commit suicide.[1] I just can't believe a god would want that to happen." Tears form in my eyes, and I look down at her plush, beige carpet. I'm bracing for a fight. In AA's world, everything is God's will. Nothing happens that God doesn't want to happen. Therefore, it was God's will that my sister Julia took her own life. I cannot accept that. But Joy nods and says something comforting. I can't remember what exactly, but it wasn't an admonishment, which is what I was expecting. Part of me knew then that if I was to believe wholeheartedly in the concept of a higher power, I would have to believe that my higher power had a reason for Julia to swallow five bottles of antidepressants. But in that moment, I can't believe that a power of good would want something so terrible to happen. And Joy doesn't force it. Which later, I realize, might have been my higher power's way of easing me into a difficult concept. If Joy had fought me on that, explained to me what I've heard later, which is that "My finite mind cannot comprehend God's infinite plan," I might have run. I might have said, "Screw this and screw AA," and then I would have picked up a drink. But that didn't happen. Joy tells me to open to page sixty in the Big Book and to read the passage starting, "The first requirement . . ."

"You are going to read the whole thing through, and you are going to read it in first person. If you get tripped up, I'll help," she says.

I start reading, pausing at the "we"s and changing them to "I"s. It is sort of fun. Instead of "Each person is like an actor who wants to run the whole show . . ." I say "I am like an actor who wants to run the whole show . . ." It is powerful, reading it like this, actively changing the point of view so that it shows how I am the root of my problems. I nod when I read "~~Is he~~ Am I not, even in ~~his~~ my best moments, a producer of confusion rather than harmony?" I'm crying by the end of it. When I get to "I am now at Step Three . . ." Joy tells me to kneel. She does too. The phrase "Hit your knees!," which I hear often in the meeting rooms, rings in my ears. I'm grateful we are in her living room on her plush carpet. On our knees, holding our Big Books in our hands, we recite the Third Step prayer together:

> God, I offer myself to Thee—to build with me and to do with me as Thou wilt
>
> Relieve me of the bondage of self, that I may better do Thy will
>
> Take away my difficulties, that victory over them may bear witness to those I would help of Thy Power, Thy Love, and Thy Way of life
>
> May I do Thy will always

DUCKS ON A POND

"Ninth Step Promise: If we are painstaking about this phase of our development, we will be amazed before we are halfway through . . . We will suddenly realize that God is doing for us what we could not for ourselves."

—*Alcoholics Anonymous*

April 2011
Three months sober

I see Chris walk up to the dugout. He looks out of place in this scene, with his long gray hair, dressed in a white oxford shirt, jeans, and blue Converse Chuck Taylors. All the other dads look the same in their Dri-FIT athletic shirts and shorts, running shoes, and baseball caps. Chris motions our son Michael over and says something through the chain-link fence. Michael fiddles with his baseball cap, snaps his Big Chew gum, and nods his head.

This is a big game for seven-year-old Michael. It's his first year in Little League and his first night game, under the lights. There is even an announcer. I want to be excited for my eldest son, but I'm annoyed about the kids being out this late. Normally, I have everyone asleep by eight o'clock. It's seven o'clock now and the game is just getting started.

I guess Chris is saying goodbye to Michael before he leaves to catch the 8:30 p.m. Amtrak train to Washington, DC, for a four-day work conference. He then walks over to Julia and Ray, who are in line at the snack bar, and gives them each a hug. Five minutes ago they asked me for money to buy a hot pretzel and I handed over some cash without reservation. I'm too emotionally drained to deal with monitoring their snack intake tonight.

Without a glance to me, Chris walks straight to his parked MINI Cooper and gets in. I shift on the cold metal bleachers. Did any of the parents notice that he didn't say goodbye to his wife? I don't think so. They are too busy watching the baseball game.

Michael comes out of the dugout to find me on the bleachers. He looks so grown up in his uniform and cleats.

"I'm pitching next inning," he says.

"Great!" I answer with forced enthusiasm.

When he turns to go back to the dugout, I put my head in my hands. What is the coach thinking? Michael's not ready to pitch. This is going to be a disaster. When I look up, I see Chris's car pull out of the parking lot. With his departure, a weight the size of a piano is lifted off my back. I take a deep breath and sit up straighter on the bench.

Chris and I had another explosive fight this afternoon. Apparently the computer's browser history was erased, and he wanted to know why. I don't know. I didn't do it. I'm not hiding anything. Not anymore, that is.

I gave Chris the same spiel I give over and over again: "My affair with Bob is over. It was only that one night. The texts and phone calls, the whole torrid episode, lasted only four months. We've had no interactions since October. I'm sorry. I love you. I want to make this work. I've stopped drinking. Please forgive me. Please please please." But when he refuses to believe me, like the flip of a switch, my pleadings turn into angry accusations. "What about you? How do I know that your emotional relationships aren't over? I saw that email from Kathy from the train. The one where she threw herself at you. When was the last time you talked to her? I know about you and Robin from work. I know you guys talked about it, considered an affair. You're not so innocent. Maybe you cleared the browser history and are blaming me to cover it up." But his affairs were only emotional, he retorts. Mine was worse because it was physical.

And that's when everything goes to shit. We try not to fight in front of the kids but it still happens. Our harsh, ragged whispers turn into fist-clenching screams and bangs on furniture. Our marriage counselor said that we are supposed to use our safe word, "daffodil," when the fighting gets out of control. Saying this word is supposed to signal us to stop and walk away from each other. We never say it.

The parents around me clap and I realize our team has the bases loaded.

"Ducks on a pond," yells an overly enthusiastic dad. *Oh no, Michael is up at bat. Oh please, don't let him strike out. That's all I ask.*

I can feel the pressure from the parents surrounding me on the bleachers. If only I was friends with one of them, I could joke about it. Make light of the situation. But I'm not friends with any of these moms. I feel so uncomfortable when I'm around them. They all seem to know each other and chat easily about school projects and town events. I can never seem to jump into their conversations, so I just sulk, off to the side.

Last year I tried to befriend one mom. Michael and her son Jimmy were in the same class and often had playdates. One time, when I came to pick up Michael from Jimmy's house, the mom was listening to the Grateful Dead while cleaning the kitchen. *I like the Dead. I have a dancing bear tattoo. Maybe we can be friends,*

I thought. After much hand-wringing over what to say and how to say it, I sent a text inviting the family over for dinner. She declined. There was an excuse, they already had plans, but I got the sense that she would never accept. In fact, a week later, she said something mean about the way Chris was dressed at the Boy Scouts Pinewood Derby. Something about how his trench coat with his hair made him look like a crazed scientist.

One day she called to invite Michael over for a playdate. I said I'd drive him over in about twenty minutes and then I poured myself a vodka cranberry. Why I couldn't wait until after Michael's playdate to drink, I don't know. In the rooms of AA, I'm learning about an alcoholic's mental obsession with and physical craving for a drink. But I'm still baffled by some of my poor choices. Did the mom smell vodka on me when I dropped him off? Did she notice I was acting differently when I picked him up a couple of hours later, after several more drinks? I'll never know. Perhaps she told the other moms in Michael's grade that I was a drunk. Maybe that's why they are so standoffish with me.

"Ball four," yells the umpire.

"Good eye, Michael," I yell.

Michael is on first base and a run came in. I breathe a sigh of relief.

I notice that my mother's Subaru has pulled into the field's parking lot. *Oh good*, I think, *now I will have someone to talk to and I won't feel so awkward.* Dressed in a long, black winter coat even though it's April, she walks slowly from the parking lot to where I am in the bleachers. I scan the bleachers to make sure she has a clear path to walk up and sit next to me. She does so very slowly. She has already broken a hip once and is careful not to trip and do it again.

"How's Michael doing?" she asks when she finally sits down next to me. I can smell the scotch cocktail she had before she left. Well, of course; it's after five-thirty. Now I wish she hadn't come. The smell of the brown liquor is simultaneously revolting and appealing. Addiction is full of these dichotomies.

"He walked and now he's on second," I answer. "There are two outs."

"Where are Raymond and Julia?"

I point to the side field, where Julia and Ray are playing on a dirt hill over behind third base, the one that looks like a termite hill. It's just a plain mound of dirt, but the kids love it for some reason. The baseball players' younger siblings who are forced to be here gather there. With no interest in the game, they run around with newly made friends, playing swords with sticks found on the ground. They are getting more exercise than the ball players, who mainly sit on the bench or stand in the field.

"Is Chris here?" my mom asks.

"He was but he left for DC."

"How long is he gone for this time?"

"Four days."

Suddenly, it occurs to me: I have the house to myself tonight. I could drink. There's that liquor store on the corner on the way home. I have cash in my back pocket. The kids wouldn't think anything of it if I said I've got to stop at this convenience store. For milk, I'll say.

In the beginners' meeting I attend on Monday nights, the old-timers would say that at this moment I should call someone to talk about my desire to drink. But if I call my sponsor, she will tell me not to drink. And I want to drink. So why would I call?

"Strike three," yells the umpire, and the parents around me clap. Oh no, Michael's team is on the field, and sure enough, Michael is on the pitching mound.

Please do well. Please do well. Please do well, I start chanting in my head. *Please don't hit the batter. Please throw some strikes.* AA says I shouldn't pray for myself. Does praying for my son count? This is what it feels like to have your organs outside of your body. I feel so vulnerable and scared and there is nothing I can do about it. It's torturous. He throws the first pitch. A ball. I can't sit here anymore.

"I'm going to check on Julia and Ray," I tell my mom. I climb down the bleachers and walk over to the termite mound. When Ray and Julia see me, they run over.

"Can we get a popsicle?" they ask in unison.

"Sure." I dig out $4 from my back pocket.

I head back to the bleachers to sit with my mom. Michael throws a strike and my mom yells, "Woo-hoo Michael! Way to go!" Her shaky, old-lady voice, emboldened by the scotch, makes me cringe with embarrassment. A woman turns around to see who yelled and I smile at her, trying to convey with my eyes, *Grandparents can be so embarrassing, right?* But the woman does not return my smile.

Finally, the game is over. My mom leaves. Michael pitched okay. He's not a superstar but he wasn't a disaster either. I gather up Julia and Ray and tell them to stay close as we are leaving. Their faces are streaked with dirt and sticky red popsicle juice. The coach has the boys in a huddle and is talking to them. Are you kidding me? Enough; we need to go home. My kids need to go to bed. I decide that if he's not done in five minutes, I'm grabbing Michael out of the huddle. I'm tired and anxious and have made the decision to do the one thing that will give me some relief: drink. I'm definitely hitting the liquor store on the way home. What's the point anyway? Chris refuses to forgive me. Who am I staying sober for? Even though I haven't taken a sip yet, the anticipation of the vodka soothes my nerves, and I can feel my shoulders drop and the tightly wound spring in my chest loosen.

After what seems like an eternity, the coach releases the players, and we all get in the minivan. Before I pull out of the spot, I check my back pocket for the cash.

Wait, where is all my cash? I have only a few crumpled dollars in my back pocket. Certainly not the $20 I would need to buy a bottle of vodka. My cluttered brain slowly realizes what's happened. I've given away all my cash to Julia and Ray, who've been buying snacks all night. I have no money left. No money to buy vodka. I'd have to get cash out of the ATM or buy a bottle with my debit card, and if I did that, Chris would know I drank. I can't have him know.

Fuck, I think, and the spring in my chest tightens again as I drive past the liquor store.

We get home and I send the kids straight to bed without a bath, something Chris would never let them do after playing in the dirt all night. They are tired and cooperate.

I contemplate my options. Is there some way to scrounge up $20 and go to the liquor store before it closes at 10:00 p.m.? It wouldn't be the first time I've left the kids home alone to run to the liquor store. Does Michael have any cash left from his First Communion? No, he spent that already. I give up. There's no way to get vodka tonight. I'll drink tomorrow. I'll get cash when I go to the grocery store, and I'll buy a bottle tomorrow. I have three more days before Chris comes home from his business trip. Three days to drink the way I want to drink without him knowing. I open the freezer, pull out three ice cream sandwiches, put them on a plate, head to the living room, and turn on the TV.

Three days later, I recount this story at the Monday night beginners' meeting. An old-timer, Tommy, chuckles when I say I ate three ice cream sandwiches instead of going out to buy a bottle.

I can feel the energy in the room connect with what I'm saying. I realize that I'm getting this now. I understand the "One Day at a Time" slogan that's plastered on placards at every meeting. I had told myself I would drink tomorrow, to make it through the night. But tomorrow came and I didn't need to drink. I am still sober. It's been three months now.

When Chris returns from his business trip, we talk. We agree that the marriage counselor is not helping, that in fact he is making things worse. We agree to continue to see our individual therapists, separately. Also, I will continue to go to AA. Chris will continue Al-Anon.

Months later, a woman named Debbie tells me how much that story touched her. How she repeats it to anyone who is not sure about a higher power.

"Huh?" I ask. I'm not sure how that story illustrates anything about my higher power.

"Your higher power did for you what you could not do for yourself. Your higher power got rid of all your cash so you didn't have money to buy vodka," she says.

Maybe, I think.

BE THE BEST WIFE I CAN BE

April 2011
Three months sober

"I can't give you relationship advice. I don't know if your marriage is going to last. But what I can tell you is that only *you* can change you"—the emphasis on "you" coming through my cell phone as bold and underlined—"you can't change him," Joy, my sponsor, says. "He has his own higher power. You are not it."

I'm standing in my kitchen, leaning against the counter and staring out the back kitchen window. The tears I've tried to stifle come streaming down my face. In the backyard, the kids' toys are strewn about—Julia's plastic buggy car and Michael's pogo stick. The kids are at school but soon I will have to pick them up.

I've called Joy reluctantly, after another fight with Chris. The fight is the same one we've had since December. It's like the movie *Groundhog Day*. The fight just repeats and repeats and there is no resolution. His accusations: Is it over? I assure him that it is. That it has been over since November. When he continues with his assault, I change tactics and accuse him. His infidelities lasted years, mine only four months. He retorts that he never acted on it. Mine is worse. Back and forth we go with no resolution ever.

"He won't forgive me," I whine to Joy. "He'll never forgive me. I think I need to leave." I pick up the coffee pot and contemplate whether it's too old to drink. I decide it's not, pour a cup into a mug, and put the mug in the microwave. Instead of vodka, I now drink old microwaved coffee all day.

"Be the best wife you can be for ninety days," Joy says. "And if things still don't look better then, we'll talk." No major changes in your first year of sobriety, she reminds me. This feels like a major change.

Inwardly I stomp my feet like a toddler unable to get what she wants.

"Fine," I say, although I know it won't work. Nothing is going to fix this shitshow of a marriage. I'll be the best wife I can be just to show Joy that it doesn't work, and then I can get the go-ahead from my sponsor to get a divorce.

What does "being the best wife I can be" even look like? I imagine myself dressed up as a fifties housewife, an apron covering my dress, in pumps and with my hair perfectly coiffed. I look down at my sweatpants and stained sweatshirt and hair that has been pulled back in a ponytail for however many days. I remember a comment Chris made to me when we still lived in Huntington. When Ray was a baby and Michael was two, my mother-in-law had invited us over for dinner and we were trying to figure out whether we should go.

"Let's just eat dinner at home," I said. "If we go to your parents', I'll have to shower and look nice."

"It might be nice if you showered and looked nice for me every once in a while," he responded.

Oh man, was I furious. Furious! Did he have any idea what it was like to take care of a newborn and a toddler all day? I barely had time to brush my teeth, much less shower and get dressed to look nice for him. But thinking about it now, I see his point. I never made any attempt to look nice for him, my husband. So I resolve to take a shower. That's one small thing I could do that actually might make me feel better. I shave my legs and even blow-dry my hair, something I normally only do for special occasions. I get dressed in capri khakis and a nicer T-shirt.

I do feel better after I shower. And even though I feel that I have nothing to apologize for, I send Chris a text: "I'm sorry we fought this morning." Period, hard stop. I don't add "Maybe if you weren't such an asshole . . ." or "Maybe you should look at yourself." I just say, "I'm sorry." And then I send another text. "Maybe we can watch *Arrested Development* together tonight." We've been binge-watching that on Netflix and both of us really love it. Chris teases me that I'm in love with Jason Bateman. I deny it but I kind of am.

I finish the rest of my microwaved coffee and get in the car to pick the kids up from preschool. My friend JaneAnn is there and asks if we want to go to the park. At the park, I don't go into my marital troubles. I'm tired of constantly talking and thinking about them. Instead, I listen to JaneAnn's issue of the day. She is frustrated with her husband's company. I mostly keep my mouth shut and just listen. Amazingly, I stop thinking about my own problems for a few minutes. Then Chris texts back: "In a meeting. Can't talk." Immediately my pilot light of anger flares up. I can hear the condescension dripping from his text: "I am the breadwinner. I can't deal with you and your petty shit during my all-important job." *Fuck off*, I think. But instead of saying that or some other snarky comment, I text back: "Okay. Well, call when you're done." I remember what my therapist constantly repeats: "It's his choice to be angry. Nothing you did can make him angry. He chooses to be angry." Fine, it's his choice, but he is choosing to be angry at me all the time. It's difficult to be around him when he's like that. I can't handle another night of getting the silent treatment in the house. I want to leave, but Joy's "Be the best wife you can be" echoes in my head.

On the way back from the park, the radio is on while the kids are in their booster seats in the back. For some reason, the news channel plays a snippet from John F. Kennedy's speech, the one in which he says: "Ask not what your country can do for you—ask what you can do for your country." How funny; it sounds like my sponsor's direction about my marriage. "Worry about yourself. Keep your side of the street clean." I hear this stuff over and over again in meetings. It's so much easier said than done. The minute Chris starts accusing me, I want to turn it all around on him. "What about you?" I always scream back. But why can't I listen to him without getting so defensive? He has a right to his fears, his worries. They are not unjustified.

When we get home, I set the kids up with a TV show in the living room. I check the computer to make sure there is nothing my father needs me to do. Nothing today. Too bad; I wouldn't mind the distraction. I hear my phone beep in the kitchen and I go to check it. Chris texts: "Can't call now, heading into another meeting. *Arrested Development* tonight sounds nice. What's for dinner?"

Usually I hate when he asks me what's for dinner. It makes me feel like a stifled housewife. But I make the decision not to let it bother me. He means no disrespect. I am the one at home, and I am the one who will shop for and make dinner. It's reasonable for him to ask that question.

"Chicken burritos," I respond.

"Yum!"

The fight is over. He is no longer angry at me. Part of me gets resentful. Why is he always the one who decides when the fight is over? But I hear Joy's voice in my head. *It's not a competition. Are you glad the fight is over? And that you didn't make it worse?*

Later, after Chris comes in the front door and the kids jump on him as a hello, he walks into the kitchen. "Something smells good," he says and kisses me on the cheek. "You look nice?" he says as a question.

"Yes, I showered," I reply and we both chuckle.

LOLLIPOPS & BLOWJOBS

May 2011
Four months sober

"Turn left onto Main Street in 450 feet." Siri's authoritative tone sounds odd coming out of my shattered old iPhone. When it fell and broke I repaired it with a screen saver, but now the protector is starting to curl at the ends and peel off. It's embarrassing, but I need the phone to last another two months until I can get a new one. We can't afford another expense.

I shut down Google Maps. I don't really need directions, but I always use the app to double-check where I am going and what time I will get there. Where is the meeting? What time is it? I check and double-check everything.

My home group is bringing a commitment to Oceanport's home group. That means members from Wednesday night go to the Sunday night meeting and speak about their "experience, strength, and hope." I'm only going for support; I didn't sign up to speak.

I do as Siri suggested and make the left onto Main Street. I spot the building where the meeting will take place: a white wharf house right on the inlet. I've driven by here a hundred times but have never noticed this meeting house. It's funny to think that all over the county people are meeting in parish houses, church basements, community houses, and their homes. In this town, there is an AA meeting practically every hour. All these people meeting, getting sober while I was home by myself drinking vodka and crying.

I pull into the parking lot and park next to Joy's minivan. I have a red Toyota Sienna. She has a blue-gray Chrysler Pacifica. Her car is nicer. She's always more put together than me. Even when we are both wearing workout clothes from Old Navy, hers fit nicely and match. Mine are baggy and stained.

I glance in the rearview mirror before I open the door. My eyes are puffy and red. I've been crying all day—yet another fight with Chris. He is always pissed off at me. This time it was because I wasn't affectionate enough. But the thing is, I've been trying, really trying to show him the love I feel in my heart. And I know that doing that means having more sex. I've been saying yes more and even initiating it. Three times a week is my goal. That's why I was so surprised when he accused me of being cold and distant.

"I'm doing the best that I can here," I yelled at Chris.

"I hate when you say that," he yelled back. "It's just an excuse."

Another big blowout in front of the kids. It seems to be getting worse instead of better. We stopped going to the marriage counselor because he didn't seem to help. In fact, we'd get even angrier after a joint session.

I grab a dollar from my purse for the basket. I decide to leave my bag in the car; no one is going to steal it and I hate it. It's so old and ratty, its frayed edges dirty with grime. I'm too embarrassed to bring it into the meeting.

I look both ways and cross the street. The sun is starting to set and the air is hazy and soft. A wave of wind crosses the cove. I always have a weird feeling right before I go into a meeting. What if someone I know drives by at this moment and sees me entering this random community house? What would they think?

Joy, Alice, and Mary are already there, sitting at a table, and luckily there is a seat next to them. Joy looks at me and I start to cry.

"What's wrong?" she asks.

But before I can answer, the leader at the podium starts the meeting. "Welcome to the Sunday night Oceanport meeting."

I shake my head and whisper, "I will tell you later."

As the leader continues with the announcement, Joy rummages through her purse. She has a nice, bright blue leather satchel. It's probably a designer purse, but I don't know anything about designers.

She pulls out a Dum Dum lollipop and hands it to me. This simple gesture is enough to make the tears stop leaking out of my eyes. She is such a mom. I take the lollipop and whisper, "Thank you." I unwrap it and pop it in my mouth and then wipe my eyes with the corner of my sweatshirt. Before I got here I thought my world was falling apart, and now, before the meeting has even started, I feel better. Like it's all going to be all right.

My sober brother Josh is the speaker: a handsome artist with a Louisiana drawl. All the women are in love with him, but he only has eyes for the guys. When he speaks, he talks about finding his higher power. He says that he didn't believe in a power greater than himself, so his sponsor took him to the beach and said, "Try to stop the waves."

"Of course, I can't," Josh responded to his sponsor.

"Well, then, there is a power greater than yourself. For now, the ocean is your higher power." And that was enough for Josh. He stopped trying to control everything and his life got better.

When the speakers are finished, everyone stands up, creates

a circle, and says the closing prayer. After thanking the speakers, Joy pulls me aside. She is shorter than me but has more of a presence. I feel mousy around her.

"What's going on?" she asks in her matter-of-fact way.

"I don't know what happened," I explain. "We were having a nice Sunday. We went to church. Then I was doing the dishes when Chris came up behind me and put his arms around me. I guess I stiffened, and he felt it. I was doing the dishes. I didn't want to have sex right then! He got frustrated with me and it blew up into a whole thing." I'm babbling I know, and I don't think I'm making sense, but she is nodding so I keep going and the tears start flowing again.

"He says I'm cold and not affectionate enough. He said I always reject him. He accused me of not being attracted to him. But that's not true," I tell Joy emphatically. "I've been trying. I've been trying to have sex more often because I know that's what he wants."

"Okay, stop right there," Joy says, holding up a hand. I've said something wrong, but I don't know what it is.

"You are not Chris's higher power, right?" she says. "You cannot fix his self-esteem. You cannot make him feel better about himself. In fact, you could get down on your knees every morning and blow him and you still wouldn't be able to make him feel better about himself."

I burst out laughing. She always has a way of making me laugh through my tears. I understand what she is trying to tell me. It's what my therapist keeps telling me: "You cannot control his feelings so stop trying to manage them. It's his choice to be angry."

"I get it," I tell her. "But it's easier said than done."

"Of course it is!" she agrees. "It's the hardest thing. Stopping drinking is easy compared to dealing with relationships sober!"

She goes on to tell me that "working the steps" is going to help me and that we need to meet next week to begin Step Four.

"Okay, I get it," I say. I grab a tissue from the box on the table and wipe at my eyes. I feel better. On the way to the meeting I was thinking about how I would get the money to pay for a divorce lawyer. But now I feel like maybe I don't have to.

When I get home, Chris is putting the kids to bed. Before I go up to say goodnight to them, I log on to the computer and go to the Fossil website. Earlier in the week I had seen a purse I liked from this company. It is more than I'd like to spend but I'm tired of feeling embarrassed by my bag. I add it to my shopping cart and complete the checkout process: a present to myself for my ninety days sober. I head upstairs to kiss the kids goodnight.

THE FOURTH AND FIFTH STEPS

Step Four: Made a searching and fearless moral inventory of ourselves.

Step Five: Admitted to God, to ourselves, and to another human being the exact nature of our wrongs.

Tuesday, May 17, 2011
Four months sober

I pull up to Joy's house and park my minivan on the street. The day is gray and the weather forecaster said to expect showers. April showers bring May flowers, but it's May now, and the showers haven't stopped. It has been a dreary spring. Several flats of annuals are laid out in the garden beds in front of Joy's house in anticipation of being planted. Today would be a good day to do it, because of the rain. I wonder if she knows that. She isn't the gardening type, I surmise. Although she has purchased plants, and I haven't even thought about spring planting at my own house. I doubt I will do any this year. I'm sober but still can't seem to get my act together.

I've arrived at Joy's house to do my Fifth Step: "Admitted to God, to ourselves, and to another human being the exact nature of our wrongs." Joy is the "other human being" and the exact nature of my wrongs is the Fourth Step I have written in a red spiral notebook with college-ruled paper. Joy told me to write out a list of resentments in columns:

I'm Resentful at . . .	*The Cause*	*Affects My*	*Character Defects*

I have written it, but I don't understand how this is going to help me discover the exact nature of my wrongs. If anything, I'm noting the exact nature of everyone else's wrongs, which I know I'm not supposed to do in AA. "Keep your side of the street clean" is what I hear in meetings all the time, which basically means I act properly, and I don't worry about whether or not the other person is acting properly. But this step focuses on other people's wrongs, specifically things that have made me angry. Joy told me to start with my mother, which made me sad because one day my kids will be listing their resentments against me.

"I tried my best," I yell into the future at my adult children's therapist.

Going in five-year increments, as instructed by Joy, I went through my life and thought about all the people, institutions, or principals that have pissed me off. It was kind of fun. "Oh yeah, and then she did that!" and "How dare he say that to me?" The last column is where I'm supposed to list my defect, how that resentment brought out selfishness, dishonesty, self-seeking, or fear. Or Joy said I could pull from the seven deadly sins, which I had to look up (so much for all those years of CCD as a kid): 1. Envy 2. Gluttony 3. Greed 4. Lust 5. Pride 6. Sloth and 7. Wrath. I don't know. I couldn't really see it. I don't know how an action someone took toward me could result in me committing a sin. Wasn't I the one who had been wronged?

I grab my notebook and my purse and walk up to Joy's front

door. The door is open so I say a tentative hello through the screen.

"Come on in," Joy says. "Let me grab my Big Book and I'll meet you in the kitchen." When I first started coming to Joy's house for step work, I was surprised that she didn't offer me coffee or a drink or put out snacks. I would never invite someone over and not brew a pot of coffee. But now I admire her indifference to normal hostess etiquette. She doesn't feel the need to please everyone all the time. It's something I'm working on.

I sit down at the table and open my notebook. She tells me to go ahead and read the resentments out loud. While I do, she empties her dishwasher. I read the first one, about my mother not paying attention to me.

I'm Resentful at . . .	*The Cause*	*Affects My*	*Character Defects*
My mother	She didn't notice that I skipped school	Security, self-esteem	Dishonest

When I'm finished, I look up from the paper at her. I raise my eyebrows and await her comments.

"What about the fifth column?" she says.

"There's a fifth column? I guess I misunderstood your instructions." I'm embarrassed by my confusion. Why can't I get anything right?

"That's okay." She waves off my embarrassment with a dish towel. "We'll do your fifth column together." She proceeds to ask me the nature of my wrong in that scenario.

"Well, I did skip school and lie to her about it."

"How come the school didn't notice?" she asks.

"The school would call after my mom left for work, and the next day I would forge an absentee note for the office. I got very good at forging my mom's signature."

"So you are mad at your mom for believing you?" She pauses

from stacking the plates to look at me. This time her eyebrows are raised.

"You disregarded the rules and lied to cover it up, you *forged* your mom's signature, and you are mad that she never noticed?"

"Oh. I see," I say, looking down at my notebook.

It goes on like this for a while. For each resentment I list, she points out what I did that was wrong. Most of the time, I was selfish or self-centered. Until this moment, I would never have described myself as selfish. In fact, when I first met Joy, I told her that I thought my problem was that I was too self*less*, that I did too much for others and not enough for myself. I needed more "self-care." I give her credit for not laughing in my face that day. As I list my resentments, I realize I had a part in the reason I felt wronged. I begin to understand the point of this exercise.

Some of the resentments make us both laugh.

"So, you are mad that your neighbors didn't ask you to watch their dog, but you said that the neighbor may have seen you drunk in the afternoon?" Joy says, her eyebrows raised in disbelief again. I put my forehead down on her table and laugh.

There are only a few in which I didn't have a part. Like:

I'm Resentful at . . .	*The Cause*	*Affects My*	*Character Defects*
My brother William	He drove drunk and died	Emotional security, personal relations	Fear, self-seeking
My sister Julia	She committed suicide and left me	Emotional security, personal relations	Fear, self-seeking

Joy assures me I didn't have part in these resentments, but she encourages me to let them go by realizing that they both were sick and suffering, William with the disease of alcoholism and Julia with mental illness. I know all this already, but it helps somehow to acknowledge it by saying it out loud to someone else. I'm allowed to have the resentment, and I'm allowed to let it go.

The whole process, me reading my resentments and Joy telling me that I'm selfish and self-centered, takes about an hour. When we finish, she explains again the reason for this exercise: resentments, more than anything, will lead us to drink. And for us, to drink is to die. We will continue to form resentments, but we can ask our higher power to remove them.

"We must or we will die," she emphasizes.

She tells me to go home and sit quietly for an hour. I agree, but I'm not sure I have time for a full hour of doing nothing. I should do some work before I get the kids from school. I decide to go for a walk on a trail in the woods near our house. It will only take thirty minutes but it's the best I can do. My kids call these woods "Two Bridges Park" because the trail crosses a stream twice and has two wooden plank bridges. When I pull up to the entrance of the trail, on a side street in a neighborhood next to the middle school, it starts to drizzle. I get out and walk anyway.

From discussions at the diner after home group, I know what comes next: my sex inventory, in which I list everyone I've had sexual relations with and my part in the ending of the relationship. *Oh boy!*

Finally spring has sprung, and it's warm and sunny on the day I read my sex inventory to Joy. We sit in her backyard, at her glass patio table, a change from the kitchen table where I normally sit and cry. I'm embarrassed as I read and I start to sweat. At one point, I look up and ask if I'm doing this right. She says I am and tells me to go on. I tell her one of my most mortifying secrets and she is nonplussed. She says, "That is on everyone's sex inventory." *It is?* I'm relieved. The result of those admissions is the same as for my resentment list. Although I often thought of myself as the victim in my past relationships, I had a part. I am not blameless in the ending of those relationships. I cheated and I lied in every serious relationship I've had.

There is one last thing to do before I'm finished with Step Five. I have to write my fear inventory. I reread the part of the Big Book that talks about fear. I think about what I'm scared about. Fear is not my thing. I'm not anxious. I don't worry needlessly. There is one major fear I have that affects my behavior and it is this: "I worry about what other people think of me." In fact, there is one story that I like to tell that accurately describes my fear versus my friend Kelly's fears. We were skiing one day, and we ended up skiing down a trail that went under the ski lift. When we got to the bottom, she said: "I hate skiing under the chair lift." I replied: "Me too! Because you are worried that people will judge your skiing abilities?"

She looked at me incredulously.

"No," she said with a chuckle, "I'm worried a chair will fall on my head and I will die." She worries she will die; I worry about what people think of me.

I write that down in my red spiral notebook. One sentence on a big, blank, lined page: *I worry about what people think of me.*

Due to our kids' hectic spring sport schedules, Joy and I can't find time to meet, so we schedule a phone date at night to go over my fears list. I assume she will balk at the fact that I have only one fear. But I tell her, and she doesn't. She listens and tells me again to go sit quietly for an hour.

"Congratulations; you have finished Step Five."

OUT OF DARKNESS WALK

Step Six: Were entirely ready to have God remove all these defects of character.

Step Seven: Humbly asked Him to remove our shortcomings.

June 4–5, 2011
Five months sober

It is midday and Chris and I smile as we pass each other in the hall. We are readying the house for our departure in a few hours—straightening up and thinking about what we will need for the walk. We are participating in the Out of Darkness Overnight Walk, a fundraiser for the American Foundation for Suicide Prevention (AFSP). Seventeen miles, from dusk to dawn, through the streets of New York City.

I have no recollection of how I became aware of this walk and the AFSP. It must have been before my sudden departure from Facebook. (I left social media soon after Chris found out about the affair. It seemed like the right thing to do.) I registered for the Overnight Walk before I stopped drinking. Before I blew up my life. I had learned that a classmate's brother had died by suicide.

My brother William was a friend of this classmate's brother, so I reached out to her and wrote a long note via Facebook messenger. I was open about Julia's suicide, maybe for the first time. It was nice to talk to someone else who had experienced the same thing. We kept in touch, and I attended a fundraiser her family threw for suicide prevention. Unfortunately I got drunk at the event. Not sloppy drunk, but still. Then I attended a Survivors' Day luncheon hosted by our local AFSP chapter. The actual lunch was boring, but it felt like a shift, like I was finally, after fourteen years, being open about Julia's cause of death.

This all happened before I stopped drinking. It was as though the seeds needed to be planted first, so that when the alcohol finally drained from my brain, the healing vines could begin to grow. But first I had to acknowledge the grief and pain without my crutch of a vodka cranberry. Even though it has been over a decade since Julia died, without alcohol to bandage my wounds, I tear up when I think of her and try to talk about her death.

I was nervous to ask Chris to join me for this walk. Things are getting better between us; the fog of anger has dissipated from our house. Joy's "Be the Best Wife You Can Be" campaign has appeared to work. At first it felt so forced to be the "best wife," to be kind and appreciative.

"Thank you for emptying the dishwasher," I'd say, even though I felt like I shouldn't have to thank him for something he should know to do anyway. But when I'd thank him for household tasks, he'd also acknowledge what I do for the family.

"Thank you for getting the kids' lunches packed and getting them to school," he'd say. I would think, *Yes, you should be thankful and you're welcome!* I was trying to be a good wife, and in turn Chris was being a good husband. Instead of keeping score about who is doing what and who is at fault for our problems, we now express our love through gratitude. Baby steps, but they seem to be working. I no longer think divorce is the answer.

However, our relationship stills feels raw and fragile. We are so cautious with each other. I was scared to tell Chris about the Overnight Walk for fear that he'd think it was just another event pulling me away from the family. But he must have sensed that this was different, that I was starting to deal with something I should have dealt with long ago. Or maybe he was just happy I was including him, opening my usual barriers enough to let him in. "Join me" is all he ever wanted me to say. When it became clear that Chris was on board for the walk through New York City, we both got excited for a night away.

Our babysitter Bethany will stay over tonight and then drop the kids off at my sister Roseann's in the morning. We will meet them there for brunch tomorrow. After we clean up the house and give Bethany directions and money for dinner, we hop in Chris's MINI Cooper and hit the road.

This, a road trip to adventure, Chris and I can do. This is our deal. We are not sure where we are going or what to expect when we get there, but we have each other. We are in it together.

"Remember that business trip to Savannah?" Chris asks.

I turn my gaze from the highway to Chris, nod, and smile.

"When my flight got cancelled? And we drove home together?" I ask.

"Yes, I still remember how you jumped up and down in the Savannah airport yelling, 'My flight's cancelled, my flight's cancelled.' You were so excited."

We both smile, remembering the road trip. We were in Savannah for a College Board conference and on the day of our return flights a storm rolled in. Chris's flight got cancelled, so instead of sitting around the airport trying to get on another flight, he was just going to keep the rental car and drive home.

He wanted me to come with him. I couldn't just not show up for my flight; the College Board had paid for it. But, if it too got cancelled, I could tell my boss I had made other arrangements and drive home with Chris. We were both thrilled when I saw the cancellation notice on the board.

Now, in his MINI Cooper on our way to Brooklyn, an unspoken question lingers: How do we get back there? Back to the point where we long to be with each other, stuck in a car with each other for twelve hours straight?

We are getting there, I think. This excursion is proof. We will drive into Brooklyn, find a place for dinner, attend an unfamiliar event, one that might make us both uncomfortable, and spend eight hours walking together through New York City. And we are choosing to do this together. We are repairing our marriage by weaving together threads of connection.

In Brooklyn, we check in at the registration desk and I'm directed to the incentive table. A man looks up my name on the spreadsheet and says, "$3,500 raised, that's excellent." I smile as I accept my swag, a baseball shirt with the "Overnight" logo on the front. I feel proud; I'm making a difference.

Next, we go to the bead table. Chris opts not to wear any. That's okay. I pick out orange, which represents loss of a sibling, as well as blue, which is general support for the cause, and at the last minute I grab green for personal struggle. This feels like a big deal, like I'm finally admitting to the world that I have suffered from depression. I understand why my sister Julia swallowed five bottles of antidepressants. I understand death as an option to escape your pain. I have been there. I know not everyone thinks like that. Chris certainly doesn't. My friend Kelly doesn't. But I do. I have thought about hanging myself, slitting my wrists, jumping off a roof. I feel something shift inside of me as I admit that.

Mariel Hemingway is the opening ceremony speaker, and I'm saddened by all the tragic losses in her family. And then the walk begins. Hundreds of us in blue shirts walk across the Brooklyn Bridge, through the South Street Seaport, up along the Hudson riverside. Texts come in from a few friends who know I'm doing this. A doctor friend who is working the night shift calls. I feel touched, connected.

At some point around mile eleven, I get annoyed with Chris. It's the constant commentary on New York. I always feel like he's trying to impress me with his knowledge. I don't always want everything to be an information dump. *You are smart*, I think. *We get it!*

As I can feel the impatience rise from my gut to my throat, where eventually it will come out of my mouth as a snap or a tone, I remember H.A.L.T. AA has taught me that we are irritable when we are Hungry, Angry, Lonely, and Tired. I'm tired. Bone tired. Unlike Chris, all-nighters are not my jam. I realize that whatever annoyance I'm feeling for Chris in this moment has nothing to do with Chris. It is me. I am tired. There is nothing I can do at this moment to fix being tired, so I need to keep my mouth shut.

Miraculously, I do. And although Chris can sense my mood of mild annoyance, I don't say anything to make it worse.

Apparently we are fast walkers because we finish early, over an hour before dawn and the Closing Ceremony. I can't bear the thought of waiting around. I'm so exhausted. Chris suggests we drive home and get a hotel room near our house. We can't go home because we'd intrude on the babysitter, so instead we drive back to New Jersey and check into the Courtyard Marriott near our home—the same hotel Chris and I used to go to when we were in the throes of our marital strife. The irony is not lost on us. We laugh about what the front desk clerk must think of us, checking into a hotel around five in the morning.

"He must think we are having an affair," Chris says. We are both too tired to care; we collapse on the bed and fall asleep until eight. Then we make love, shower, and go to my sister's to grab the kids.

"How was it?" Roseann asks when we arrive. She hands me a cup of coffee and I sit down at her kitchen table. Julia climbs in my lap.

"It was good. I'm sore for sure. But it was good."

And I do feel good. I feel like I've done something important, not only for suicide prevention, not only in memory of my sister Julia, but also for myself. And I've included Chris. I've lowered my walls.

FIRE ISLAND

August 9–12, 2011
Seven months sober

Chris is weaving the minivan between the cars on the Belt Parkway. I glance at the TomTom GPS system. When I set it up, Chris got annoyed.

"We don't need that. I know the way."

"I know, I just like to see which route it will take us," I say defensively, and add, "11:10 a.m. arrival," trying to make my voice sound matter-of-fact instead of accusatory. We lost ten minutes when Chris pulled over at a rest stop to check that the bikes were secure on the bike rack, a move I felt was overly cautious.

"It's fine. We are paying them. They will wait for us."

I hate being late, even if we are the customer and probably do have some wiggle room in our water taxi pickup time.

I am agitated and annoyed. I feel prickly and try to say the "Serenity Prayer" in my head to make it go away. It doesn't work. Chris planned this ridiculous, unnecessary trip and then barely helped to get us out the door. I'm the one who made sure the kids all had bathing suits that fit and thought about our meals and what food we should bring.

I turn and look at the kids in the back. The boys' heads are bent over their Nintendos. Julia is happily sucking on her blanket and staring out the window. They are quiet. Probably because Chris and I were snapping at each other as we packed and cleaned the house. It's a lot to plan for. Food on the island is super expensive, so we try to bring as much as we can. Then, of course, there's all the kids' stuff, buckets and boogie boards. In later years, the kids will declare the day we leave for our annual Fire Island vacation "the most stressful day of the year." And it might have been this year that set the tone.

This is our second year of venturing to Fire Island for a weeklong vacation. Fire Island is a thin barrier island off the southern shore of Long Island. It's known for protected beaches interspersed with seasonal resort communities.

At first, I was against Chris's Fire Island vacation plans. He'd show me potential houses to rent online and I'd respond with a shrug and say, "We live at the Jersey Shore. Why would we pay money to rent a beach house?" But when Chris gets a notion in his head, he is persistent. His argument was that Fire Island is a unique place with no cars, where you can ride your bike around. And, because it's an island far out in the Atlantic, the ocean is cleaner and clearer.

"It's just special. You'll see," he concluded.

And even in my alcoholic fog last year, I did see what he meant. The kids stretched their independence by riding their bicycles from our rental house into town and back again. It was a beach resort, but it had a city-like feel. It had an edge to it. I liked it.

Now that I am sober and trying hard to be a better wife, I realize that, for whatever reason, Chris really wants his family to spend a week on Fire Island again.

"You're complaining because your husband wants to plan a

family vacation. Are you kidding?" Joy has said. So here we are again on what will become an annual trip to Fire Island. We are renting a different house this year, one closer to the town.

But as our departure date neared, I began to think about what it would be like to be on a weeklong beach vacation without drinking, especially in a spot that's known for its partying. The saying "Toes in the sand, drink in the hand" is plastered on every T-shirt and mug across the island. Beach vacation equals drink vacation. I've never gone on a trip without enjoying cocktails to help get in the vacation mood.

A few days before we leave, I share my worries at the Monday night beginners' meeting. There is not supposed to be any cross talk, but the people with more time than me give me advice. Use your phone, keep in touch with your network. Research the meetings ahead of time and schedule them. Think the drink through. One predinner cocktail for me will lead to me sneaking vodka cranberries all day.

With Chris's aggressive driving, we gain back the ten minutes and arrive at the taxi dock at exactly 11:00 a.m. Chris points at the clock and says triumphantly, "Right on time!" *See, you stressed about nothing!* Joy's voice says in my head. We are all hot and sweaty by the time we unload from the car all the bikes and bags of food and clothes for the week and load everything onto the boat that is our personal taxi. The water taxi is definitely a better way to cross the bay than the ferry. I'm grateful Chris had the foresight to book it. Finally, after lugging everything out of the car and onto the boat, Chris goes off to park the car in the lot. We all get on the boat and sit on the bench in the back. As the boat departs Bay Head and heads across Great South Bay to Ocean Beach Fire Island, I feel the wind blow away my stress and agitation. Maybe this will be a nice trip after all.

At the Ocean Beach dock we do the haul in reverse, pulling

everything off the boat and then dragging it all piecemeal to the house we rented.

"It's 329 Duenhoff," Chris says, and the kids take off on their bikes to find it.

When we arrive, the former renters are just leaving. They are hungover twenty-year-olds dragging their feet for their checkout. We, the family with three young kids, are early for our check-in. Chris calls the rental manager and makes it clear that the previous renters need to clear out so we can move in. We tell the twenty-year-olds we are going to check out the beach, to give them time to pack up their stuff. The subtle hint: "When we get back, you'd better be gone." I feel my agitation kick up a notch. Why are we subjecting ourselves to this unnecessary stress? The old refrain, *Why are we doing this when we live at the beach?*, pops back in my head.

At the beach, the kids run across the sand and splash in the surf. Again, my agitation is blown away by the ocean air. Chris grabs my hand as we trail behind the kids. He smiles at me with a look that says, *See? This will be fun. I promise.*

The kids are getting hungry for lunch, so we head back down to the house, passing a large but mangy-looking doe on the way, which we all pause to gawk at. Fire Island is known for its deer population, which roams among the tightly packed houses. When we get to our rental, the twenty-somethings are gone, thank God.

I start to lug our grocery bags into the house's kitchen, then I stop short. There, in the middle of the counter, I'm confronted with a large bottle of Grey Goose vodka. It's tall and elegant and appears to grow larger as I stare at it. I turn on my heels and walk outside. Chris looks at my face and says, "What?" *What now*, he is thinking.

"Vodka. On the counter."

Chris jumps into action. He grabs the bottle and starts dumping it down the sink. I say, "Wait wait, don't waste it! It's a full bottle." Which is ridiculous. Why am I concerned with wasting the vodka? He tells me to go outside while he deals with the bottles all over the counter.

I do. I go outside and without a thought I do something I'm not typically willing to do: I call my sponsor, Joy. I don't think about it until later, but I realize all those daily calls I made when nothing was happening made it second nature to pick up the phone when I really needed something. While pacing up and down on the sandy sidewalk, I explain to her about the vodka on the counter. Joy talks about going to a meeting.

"There are always great meetings in locations where there is typically a lot of drinking," she says. She gets Alice on the phone, who is able to find where and when the meetings are. Alice emails me the list. I realize I've screwed up by not researching the meetings beforehand, like I had been told to do. I'm grateful for my friend and her computer. She has found me a meeting to attend tomorrow night. Knowing that I will be going to a meeting here settles me a bit.

I go back into the house and Chris has either dumped or stored away all the leftover alcohol from the twenty-year-olds.

"Who would abandon a practically full bottle of Grey Goose?" I say to Chris.

"Not you!" Chris says with a smile, and we both laugh.

The kids have claimed their rooms and explored the whole house and they are already ready for the next adventure: heading into town for ice cream.

"No rest for the weary," Chris says. He will take them to get ice cream if I want to unpack the groceries. "You okay in the house?" he asks.

"I'm okay."

And I am okay after talking to Joy and Alice. I have a plan to go to a meeting on Wednesday, which is perfect because that's when my home group meets.

On the day of the meeting, I tell Chris I'm nervous. Chris doesn't understand this side of me, this fragile mush of a person who has trouble functioning in society. He is always confident around strangers, thrives on meeting people even. I avoid new places and new people.

"Where's the meeting?" he asks, and I tell him.

"I'll go with you. I mean I'll ride over there with you."

We ride our bikes to the small church. I see a few other bikes by a side door and realize that's probably where the meeting is held. I park my bike next to the others and Chris gives me a kiss and says, "See you in an hour."

The following day I see the leader of the meeting on the beach and I point him out to Chris.

"That guy was in the meeting." I am comforted to see sober people out in this "toes in the sand, drink in the hand" world. Also, having Chris support me, first by rushing to get rid of the alcohol bottles and then by leading me to the meeting, makes it feel like we are in this together. I'm not alone in my recovery. He is by my side as I "trudge the road to happy destiny."[1]

APOLOGIES GONE AWRY

Step Eight: Made a list of all persons we had harmed, and became willing to make amends to them all.

Step Nine: Made direct amends to such people wherever possible, except when to do so would injure them or others.

September 30, 2011
Eight months sober

I turn the wheel sharply to the right to park the minivan in the visitor parking lot of my parents' condo complex. There are only five narrow spots and I never get the car in properly on the first try. I open my door and look down, and sure enough, I'm over the white line. Closing the door, I then reverse and straighten it out and pull back into the spot. I do this carefully because last week I turned on an angle and hit the corner of the retaining wall, putting a small dent and scratch in the panel of the sliding passenger door. I couldn't believe it! I've parked here practically once a day for the last three years. This minivan messes with my spatial perception. I hear my sponsor's voice say, "You have a disease of perception." And I giggle to think it even applies to my parking ability. About a year ago, I dented the bumper of Chris's

MINI Cooper while backing out of our driveway. And apparently I didn't handle the situation correctly because I received the silent treatment from Chris for several days.

"It was an accident," I explained to Chris after I couldn't take the silence anymore. "Why are you so mad?"

His feeling was that I didn't take the dent seriously enough. I told him in an offhand way, as a second thought, and my apology was cavalier.

I remember saying, "My dad always taught me not to sweat the small stuff."

"Denting my car isn't small stuff!" Chris shouted at me through the phone. But it was to me. That's one of the main differences between me and Chris. I just don't care about that kind of thing. I don't know if it's the result of having dealt with real, serious tragedies growing up, but things like dented cars aren't a big deal to me. A crashed car with a dead brother inside, now that's a big deal. Or maybe it has nothing to do with those tragedies. Maybe I'm missing some gene and that makes me unconcerned or irresponsible. I used to think I was super laid-back, but after doing my Fourth Step, I know that isn't an accurate description. I'm unconcerned about some things but I'm hypersensitive about other things.

I learned from my mistake last year, so this time, after the accidental denting, I immediately called Chris. I knew I couldn't fake sounding distraught over the accident. That would have been insincere. Instead I said, "I know it's important to you to drive the family around in a nice-looking car, so I'm very sorry this happened." And things went smoothly. We are learning.

Before getting out of the car, I grab my purse and make sure I have my printed script and my cell phone. I am making my amends to my mother today. Before heading into my parents' condo, I dial Joy and walk down the driveway towards the river. Although I see this view every day, I never get tired of it. Their condo sits at the base of a river. They have the best view on the peninsula because they don't look toward either bank but upriver toward a distant bridge. It is late September and there is a new autumn chill in the air. The warm water collides with the crisp air, creating a fine mist that hovers over the water. I hear the shout of a dock worker at the nearby hotel. They are dry-docking the boats for the season. My dad's sailboat is still at their dock. He hasn't had the time to use it much this summer and is hoping to get in some sailing before the end of the season.

The phone rings in my ear and I take a deep breath while staring at the water, to settle my nerves. I've come to this river my whole life to pause and recenter myself. When I was younger, I would walk to this river from my house. I'd sit on top of the concrete sewer drain and gaze out onto the salty waterway. I dreamed of building a raft, like Huck Finn, and floating away from it all. Or I'd pick out rocks from the muddy sand and pitch them as far as I could, to hear them go *plop* in the river, while contemplating why my best friend never called. The day after my brother died, I walked down to the river to escape the silence in my house.

"This is Joy. Leave a message," says my sponsor's voicemail. I didn't expect her to pick up. She rarely does these days. And she won't call back unless I specifically ask.

"Hi, Joy. It's Liz. I'm about to do the amends to my mom and I'm following instructions and calling you beforehand. I'll call you when it's over."

Okay, that's done. I pull myself away from the river and head up the hill to my parents'. I resist the urge to pick up the pine cones scattered along the path to the front door. I have a thing for pine cones, but once I've collected them, I rarely do anything with them. I have no follow-through. So I try to stop picking them up because they just end up causing a mess in the minivan. I enter through the kitchen door and yell, "Hello!" No answer. I knew my dad would be gone. He is at a hearing in New York. It's why I picked this day to make amends to my mom. We'll be alone in the house. My mom must have run out to do an errand, so I will have to wait. I check my work basket, where I find several receipts. I need to compile an invoice for my dad. I'm glad I have something to distract me, a task I can get done. I head upstairs to my dad's office to work. I pass my favorite painting on the landing. The artist was a friend of my grandmother's, I think. She made a painting of a photo of my grandmother at the beach in a bathing suit, holding the hands of my sister Julia and brother William when they were toddlers.

I wonder who will get the painting when my parents die. Roseann and I will both want it for sure. It represents our childhood: our grandmother bringing us to the beach, teaching us how to swim. And, of course, it has our two late siblings. I remember when my grandmother died, about a year after my sister Julia and eight years after my brother, and there was some discussion about who would get the painting. My mom's response was, "Are you kidding? Of course it's mine. Those are my children in the painting." But between me and Roseann, ownership won't be as obvious, and we will both want the painting. I imagine us in this condo, going through all their possessions, deciding what to keep, sell, or give away. We come to this painting, get in a huge fight, and don't talk for several weeks. *Really?* my sponsor says in my head. She is exasperated with me. *We are worried about something that isn't going to happen for years? Let's just focus on today, and the amends to your mom. We will worry about who gets what when they die when it happens.*

Okay, okay, I tell the Joy voice in my head, and I log on to my dad's computer to do my work. About twenty-five minutes later I hear the whirring motor of the garage door opening. My mom's home. I finish up the invoice I'm working on, save it to come back to later, and go downstairs.

"Need any help bringing in bags?" I yell down the stairs to the garage.

"Yes," my mom says. Her tone is always harsher than she means it to be. I'm used to it but it can rub people the wrong way. I meet her in the garage, where she is slowly making her way inside.

"I stopped at the grocery store after getting my blood checked," she says. "There are bags in the back." I grab the two paper grocery bags, bring them upstairs, and place them on the kitchen table.

"How are the kids?" my mom asks when she finally makes it up to the kitchen.

"They are good," I reply with my standard response. "They are all at school."

After the groceries get put away I can no longer stall, because if I do, I won't go through with it. I know that much. Like calling Chris after denting the minivan, I've got to do this promptly.

"Mom, can I talk to you a minute?" I say. "Come sit with me here in the living room."

My mom is panicked. A mother who has lost two of her four children, she fears the worst. I quickly assure her it's for something good, not something bad. We sit formally in the living room. She is in the armchair facing the glass sliding doors that look out over the river. I'm on the couch facing her. I pull out the printed script from my purse and she really looks confused. I explain that as part of my Twelve-Step program I need to make amends for my wrongs.

"No no no," she waves her crooked arthritic hand at me. "You don't have to do this." I explain that I have to and I just plow ahead, reading straight from the script. I don't look up and make eye contact. It's too difficult. I read the items straight through without pause, my voice shaking.

- I skipped school in seventh and eighth grade without your knowledge. I would pretend to go to school and then sneak in the basement windows and wait for you to go to work. I would then forge your signature on my absentee notes the next day. I continued that practice throughout high school.
- Starting around fourth grade and probably until my early twenties, I would steal money out of your purse.
- Starting from eighth grade until last December, I would steal alcohol from your liquor cabinet.
- I would lie or make excuses when you would find evidence of my drinking in high school. I would never take responsibility for my actions.
- In high school, I would lie about where I was going.
- I often threw parties at your house. I had a total disregard for your property and household rules. When confronted, I would lie about who was at the house.
- I embarrassed you by continuously getting in trouble. I remember one particular time when I threw up on the steps of Nativity Church on the way into Midnight Mass on Christmas Eve.
- I wasted your money by not committing myself to college. I stopped going to Brookdale after you paid for my class registration. At St. Michael's, I didn't apply myself to the best of my ability. I failed several classes. To make up for those classes, I had to go to summer school and attend an extra semester at college. You paid for those classes.

- I had a general disregard for any type of authority and was disrespectful when questioned about my behavior. I remember the time you found the fake ID I had made with Roseann's birth certificate. You rightly cut it up and I was unjustifiably angry.
- While at St. Michael's, I crashed the Volvo while I was intoxicated, and I lied about the circumstances of the crash. You paid to fix the car.

My mom nods her head as I read and accepts my apology for all my wrongs. We are both crying now, and she insists it's all right.

"I'm so glad that you are doing well now. I'm so proud of you," she says. She wants this to be over. She does not like dredging up the past.

We hug awkwardly. She is so frail that I can only gently rest my arms around her shoulders. I fear any more pressure would break her in two.

The air is heavy, uncomfortable. I decide to pack it up and finish any work I have to do from my computer at home.

As I start to leave, she says, "I'm sorry if I didn't pay enough attention to you when you were younger. I didn't know you were skipping school and going back into the house through the basement windows."

"It's okay, Mom. I'm sorry for all the things I did," I assure her, and quickly walk outside.

I immediately smell the river, a mix of fish and salt, and it hits me. I've fucked up the amends. I broke one of the rules: don't say anything that would hurt or harm them. I wasn't supposed to apologize for something that she didn't know about, that would hurt her. The first amends I made were things she didn't know. I don't know how I didn't notice that before.

I'm shocked when I realize my duplicity. I've felt hurt my whole life, wanting more attention from my parents, wanting somebody to notice how hurt and damaged I was. When I did my Fourth and Fifth Steps, I was supposed to have gotten that resentment out and come to terms with it, realizing that my parents were doing the best they could. As a parent myself I can understand that. But I guess I wasn't over it. Part of me didn't want to just say an amends to my mom. Part of me wanted an apology from her. And I got it. Now she feels bad for her wrongs, but that is not what this is about. I've totally fucked this up and any good feeling about making amends to my mom is now tainted with this knowledge. Walking back to my minivan, I pick up the phone to call Joy. Voicemail again.

"Hi, Joy. It's Liz again. Just calling to say I made amends to my mom. It went well," I say. She doesn't call me back and I don't mention the screwup.

Five years later, on an AA retreat, after the leader discusses Step Nine, I reveal my mistake to my sponsor.

"I purposefully told my mom something that I knew she didn't know, to make her feel bad for not paying enough attention to me," I say. "Well, not purposefully, but subconsciously. I didn't realize I had included that in my amends until after I read it to her." I try to explain how one part of my brain acted independently of the other and hid this hurtful jab at my mother until it was too late.

"Do I go back now and say an amends for messing up her amends?" I ask, but I know the answer. I've been around long enough to know what my sponsor is going to say. I've heard her in my head for years.

"You make a living amends to her every day. She is so grateful for all that you do for her. You are a good daughter now. There is no reason to revisit that."

And I know that. I know that I show up unselfishly for my mom pretty much every day: taking her to her doctor's appointments, helping with tasks around the house that she can no longer do, like bringing in groceries or taking the garbage out. Whatever mistake I made five years ago when making my amends is long forgiven.

RENEWING OUR VOWS

October 2011
Nine months sober

I pull out a large white box from underneath my bed. It's covered in dust, and I immediately break out in a sneezing fit due to my dust mite allergy. The sneezing doesn't abate and I'm forced to splash water on my face to recover. In the box is my mother's wedding dress. It's also my wedding dress. Ten years ago I tried on my mother's wedding dress at my parents' condo, about a month before my wedding.

"Well, this fits. That's done," I declared on that day, checking another thing off my list. The only alterations I made were having the sleeves removed.

Chris and I got engaged at the end of August 2001, and then September 11th happened. I don't need to explain here what it was like in New York City at that time. You can imagine, or maybe you were there. After that horrific event, Chris and I saw no need to wait a whole year to begin our life. If there is a good thing about tragedy—and I unfortunately know from too much experience—it's that it is a wake-up call to what's important in life: your loved ones. Also, if we wanted Chris's Jesuit uncle to marry us, we needed to marry while he was still stateside, before he returned to his mission in Africa. With international travel precarious due to the terrorist attacks, who knew if he'd ever be coming home? So we declared that we'd get married in October, and we miraculously pulled together a wedding in a month. When I went to tour the reception space on the Jersey Shore in Sea Bright, NJ, I looked out the window towards the city and saw plumes of smoke billowing from Ground Zero.

That is why, when I tried on my mother's wedding dress on that day and it fit, I was ready to check that off my list and move on to the next task.

I try it on now in our messy bedroom. Again, I am amazed that it fits. Would it be weird to wear it to our vow renewal? It's not weird to wear it for the ceremony. I see lots of weddings take place on the beach. But what about at the restaurant afterwards, me in my wedding dress while everyone else is just there for a casual dinner?

Who cares, I decide. What is it my AA people are always telling me? "It's none of your business what other people think of you."

I go through the checklist. Corsages ordered. Dinner reservations made. Bethany on board to babysit the kids after the ceremony. Limo rented. Hotel room booked. And now outfit planned. I'm surprised at all the traditional wedding things we've opted for. Things like corsages and limos are not important to me. But I want this vow renewal ceremony to feel like a legitimate wedding. I want to do it right. Or, as Chris keeps saying, this is our chance to recommit. We had a chance to leave. The door was open for both of us, and we decided not to. So, once we renew our wedding vows in a ceremony on the beach officiated by JaneAnn's pastor husband Adam, that option, divorcing, is off the table. We will stop using it as a threat every single time we get in a fight. Or at least that's the plan.

I'm nervous on October 8, the day of the ceremony. Why, I'm not sure. One of the reasons is that I feel guilty for not inviting my parents or my sister to this event. I barely told my AA people. To this day, over ten years later, it makes me uncomfortable to think about this omission. If I am to give myself an excuse for not inviting them, it would be that sometimes my family feels too damaged. We come with so much baggage. Sometimes I want to put all that aside. Be someone different. Not be the person who lost two siblings to alcohol and mental illness. Or maybe that's bullshit, maybe it's more because I don't want to highlight how I screwed up my marriage so badly that we need to renew our vows. Or it might be more simple. By six o'clock, the time of the ceremony, I know my mother will have several scotches in her. And maybe I just don't want to deal with that on this day that's about fresh starts.

We opt to invite only a few core people who have been on this yearlong roller coaster ride with us: JaneAnn and Adam, whose religious faith has helped us find our higher power. Kelly and Scott, our forever friends. And Chris's sister Angela and her husband Rainer, who helped us with advice during this rocky period. Michael, Ray, and Julia will come to the beach for the ceremony; Bethany will be in charge of them. After the ceremony, they'll ride home in the limo and the adults will go out to eat.

The afternoon is flying by as all of us in the house are getting dressed in our fancy clothes. We are running behind schedule. I'm frantic that we are going to miss the sunset. That was one of my main goals: to say our vows during sunset, because it's such a beautiful time. Of course, the sun doesn't set on the ocean in New Jersey, but still the light will be beautiful. And the photos will be amazing.

Despite being behind schedule, we get there in the nick of time. The light is beautiful. Adam says the proper exchange. Chris and I each read our prepared vows.

I wish I could remember them. Perhaps they live somewhere on an old laptop. But I remember the gist: We both described a new beginning forged in honesty; the love was always there, but love is not enough. We committed to a willingness to accept each other for who we are. We committed to saying we are sorry and to forgiving each other. We committed to always working to better ourselves. We committed to each other.

After the ceremony, we walk to McLoone's restaurant for our dinner reservations. The meal is mediocre. This restaurant is known for its view of the ocean, not its fine dining. I get up to go the bathroom and notice a few people glance at me. Are they judging me for being in a wedding dress while the rest of the restaurant is barely wearing flip-flops? I decide I don't care. And I recognize this feeling: it's the same feeling I get after two drinks. The *I'm happy, I'm confident, I feel good* feeling. I'm amazed that I feel this way without alcohol. *Cherish this feeling*, my sponsor would say, *because it won't last.*

FIRST SOBER THANKSGIVING

November 2011
Ten months sober

It's the Wednesday night before Thanksgiving and the mood in the Christ Church parish house is jovial. All of us alcoholics are happy to be at our home group meeting the night before we sit down at a table to eat turkey with the people who drove us to drink. It amuses me to think we are all here at an AA meeting on one of the biggest bar nights of the year. But, of course, I stopped going to bars in my late twenties anyway and would just drink at home alone.

The guest speakers (we call them "the commitment") are middle-aged, two men and a woman. The leader opens with: "I'm very unique. I'm an Irish Catholic from Jersey City," which gets a laugh because there are a ton of Irish Catholics from Jersey City in AA. Too bad he is not the main speaker because he seems entertaining.

"Leaders lead and speakers speak," he says and introduces the first speaker, John, a balding biker with tattoos peeking out of his ratty gray T-shirt. I zone out during John's share. Even though I'm not supposed to compare, I can't relate to his story, which describes one DWI after another. I think by the third arrest for drinking and driving, I might have admitted I had a problem. Not this guy! Plus, I am distracted by Carrie, who is scrolling through Facebook on her cell phone while sitting in the front row, right in front of the podium and the speaker. She's so rude. To resist the urge to swat the phone right out of her hand, I chant the "Serenity Prayer" several times in my head.

Thankfully, Carrie puts away her phone when the woman speaker gets up to the podium. I can relate to this woman's story. She explains how she would do a household project, like paint a room, and then reward herself with a bottle of champagne. My story is similar. I would take the kids to an activity, like the Bronx Zoo, and then reward myself with vodka when we got home. However, because alcoholism is a progressive disease, toward the end of my drinking, I would reward myself *before* the activity. I cringe with guilt and shame when I think about the time I took them to the beach after a few drinks. Would I have been able to save them if they had gotten in trouble in the ocean? Luckily I never had to find out.

The meeting is over, and everyone gets in line to thank the speakers. Afterwards, we mill about asking about each other's plans for the holiday.

I'm anxious about Thanksgiving, my first one sober. Not so much worried that I'm going to drink, but about how I am going to survive my family without drinking. Already there is an issue with my sister Roseann, whose feelings are hurt because my mom is hosting Thanksgiving at our country house in Pennsylvania. Roseann can't come because her husband, a high school athletic director, works on Thanksgiving. Roseann won't leave him behind, even though I'm sure he wouldn't care. My sponsor Joy says to stay out of it. It's not my place to make suggestions. A couple of days ago, I called Roseann to ask what she was doing for Thanksgiving. She didn't pick up so I left a voicemail.

She emailed me back and said she didn't want to talk about it because her feelings are hurt. Whenever I think about my sister being mad at me, my stomach lurches and I start to sweat. I want to make everything better, explain to Roseann that she doesn't need to be so pissed off. But Joy keeps telling me that there is nothing I can do about it. All I can do is keep my side of the street clean. I picture myself with a broom, on a sidewalk next to a street with sparkling blacktop. On the other side of the yellow line is my sister with her arms crossed, garbage everywhere, glowering at me.

After I shake the hands of the speakers, I look around the room to find Joy. She is talking to Carrie, hopefully scolding her for having her phone out at a meeting. I wait behind Carrie, making it obvious that I need to talk to Joy. Alice gets behind me. We are all lining up to talk to our sponsor the night before Thanksgiving. Around us, people are putting away the chairs and sweeping the floors.

"Well, that's why we have a party on January 2nd. If we survive the big three, Thanksgiving, Christmas, and New Year's, without picking up a drink, we alcoholics celebrate on January 2nd," Joy tells Carrie, and turns to include me in the conversation. "Alice is hosting it this year. I hope you can come." She makes it sound fun, like we are all in this together and we just need to survive until January 2nd, when we can breathe a sigh of relief and get back to our lives.

Carrie leaves and I get to talk to Joy alone for a moment. I explain that I'm nervous that everyone will be drinking in this small country house. My cousin and her husband who are coming from Vermont are heavy drinkers. And of course there's my mom and her scotch. Joy tells me that her sponsor would always tell her that when she is feeling uncomfortable, she should do the dishes.

"Whenever you are feeling squirrelly," Joy says, "and you're not sure what to do with yourself, go do the dishes. There are always dishes to do on Thanksgiving."

"And then call Sue," Joy continues. "She's sitting at home all alone. Joe will have the kids. She has no family. She will be sitting in her house by herself on Thanksgiving. It'll be a miracle if she doesn't drink. It's not good," Joy says.

I nod my head and try not to look wistful at the thought of being all by myself on Thanksgiving, drinking vodka in an empty house.

I know I'm supposed to feel sorry for this woman, a mother of school-age children who can't put down the drink. She was sent away to rehab for six months! Six months and she still can't stay sober. I would never admit it to anyone, but part of me is envious. I never had this epic battle with alcoholism. Scratch that. I had an epic battle, but it was all waged in my head. No one else witnessed it. I feel like I missed out on some alcoholic rite of passage.

I know I should be grateful I didn't get sent to rehab, that I could stay home and be a mother to my kids. But part of me wishes I had gone to rehab. I could have concentrated on getting sober, instead of getting sober while still working and dealing with the kids.

As usual, everyone is going to the diner after the meeting, but I opt to go home. My excuse is that I have to leave early in the morning for Pennsylvania.

The next morning, Thanksgiving morning, Chris and I pack up the car and the kids by eight o'clock. We should get there around eleven. As soon as we get on the highway, I put on our CD of *Alice's Restaurant* by Arlo Guthrie. The kids don't understand the song, but they like the tradition of us playing it. As they get older, they remember these holiday traditions and ask for them each year. The car ride is uneventful. The leaves have yet to fall off the trees in New Jersey and I gaze at the scenic landscape zooming by.

I think back to our car ride to Chris's family in Long Island last year. Chris and I had gotten in a huge fight. I don't remember what about. He hadn't even found out about the affair yet, so it wasn't about that. I just remember feeling suffocated by the fog of hate in our minivan on the Long Island Expressway. I'm sure I was pissed off because I felt like I had to do everything—make a dessert to bring to dinner, get the kids dressed and ready to go. Chris was probably sick of me being a bitch all the time. We weren't speaking when we arrived at my sister-in-law's house, and I went straight to the bar to make myself a drink. My sisters-in-law were drinking too, so I didn't feel conspicuous with a vodka cranberry in my hand. After several stiff drinks, I tried to make peace with Chris. I gave him a kiss and said I loved him. He returned the kiss but said, "I don't need alcohol to know that I love you." I felt like I had been sucker punched in the gut. Tears came to my eyes, and I said something bitchy back. And that's basically how the rest of the night went. It wasn't surprising that a few short weeks later our life imploded.

On this car ride, I grab his hand while Arlo sings about sitting on the bench, on the "group w" bench. I feel a wave of gratitude to be together with my husband and three kids on the way to the country. He feels it too; he brings my hand to his mouth and tenderly kisses it. I am a different person than I was last year. I may still want to drink, but I don't want to go back to being that resentful, pissed-off bitch. I don't want to fight with Chris. Renewing our vows last month sealed the deal. We had the chance to get out of the marriage, but we've recommitted ourselves. This is it. It's a new marriage. That's the plan, anyway.

We arrive at the Farm. That's what my family calls this century-old house in the boondocks of the Endless Mountains. Most of the other guests, my parents and my cousins, are already there. It's nice to be greeted by a big crowd, and I haven't seen my cousin Eileen and her family in a long time. After we unpack and settle in, we all go for a walk in the woods. My mother has named all the trails and marked them with burn-engraved wooden signs. Up the hill to the Cowboy Tree, then across Dinosaur's Back and up to the Bear Caves, and across to Trillium Ridge and back down to the dirt road. When I get a chance to be alone with my cousin Eileen, I make my amends to her. It's basically, "Sorry I was such an inconsiderate house guest when I lived with you in college."

She brushes it off with a wave of her hand, dismissing me. "You were twenty years old. That's how twenty-year-olds act." Next, I corner her husband, Charlie. He takes my amends a little more seriously. He gives me a hug and says he's proud of the changes I'm making. These amends are uncomfortable to make but I'm glad I can now check them off the list. I only have one or two more to do.

Charlie organizes a touch football game in the field next to the house. I don't like games that have the potential to lead to the kids fighting, so I go inside to see if my mom needs any help in the kitchen. She and Eileen are leaning against the counters, chatting away and sipping from small glasses of scotch. I usually love being around my mom while she is cooking, but today the fumes from the scotch are making me twitchy inside. There are no dishes to do, so I take a walk outside and look at the trail up to the Cowboy Tree. It could use some clearing. I find some "shovels and rakes and implements of destruction," as Arlo would say, in the upper barn. I bring them to the head of the trail and begin hacking away at the briar bushes. A large, half-buried rock makes the trail bumpy. I grab the shovel and dig all around the rock until it's loose enough to roll out of the hole. I put it on the side of the trail. Then I notice another half-buried rock in the path. I dig out that rock. I keep digging out rocks until the football game is over. I'm covered in sweat and dirt and have realized that, instead of making a nice smooth trail, I've created large, dangerous holes in it. I learn later that the holes collect water when it rains and make the trails a muddy mess. It's time to shower and get ready for Thanksgiving dinner.

The weekend ends and I can't say that I had a good time sober at this Thanksgiving. But I've made it through without picking up a drink or picking a fight with anyone. And Chris and I are still talking. Joy would say I now have a "sober reference." I've done this activity sober, so I know I can do it again. Which is good, because Christmas is right around the corner.

A DESK AND DESPAIR

Step Ten: Continued to take personal inventory and when we were wrong promptly admitted it.

February 2012
One year and one month sober

The despair is back. It's so familiar that its return is almost comforting, like seeing an old friend, until you remember that friend is misery. I am miserable.

It is mid-February. I have made it through the big three without incident: Thanksgiving, Christmas, and New Year's Eve. My sober family had a party on January 2nd to celebrate getting through the holidays without a drink and with a minimal amount of amends. I celebrated one year sober on January 8. Amazing!

Things were going well until they weren't. I wasn't blindsided by these feelings of despair. Like I said, this is familiar to me. A part of me feels victorious: *This is how you really are. Stop pretending you're happy, joyous, and free. This miserable SOB is the real you.*

A deep anguish causes a throbbing tightness in my chest. The feeling reminds me of a toy my kids have. "Award-winning geometric expanding/contracting ball," the Amazon description said when I purchased it for Christmas. If you pull the plastic rods out, the toy expands to a foot-long sphere. But then, if you push the rods together, it contracts to a five-inch ball. My chest is stuck inside that plastic contraption, and I can't figure out how to pull the rods the right way so that it will expand and I can be released from this pain. All I want to do is make this feeling go away. The contracting ball makes me feel like I can't breathe properly, and I keep sighing in an attempt to loosen the tightness.

"What's wrong, Mom?" six-year-old Raymond asks when he catches one of my sighs over breakfast one morning. I'm afraid Ray has inherited my sensitivity, which I know through doing the Fourth and Fifth Steps with Joy is a selfish defect, always worrying about other people's moods, always worried that you are the cause of their bad mood. I smile at him and assure him it's nothing, I'm just overwhelmed.

Nothing is wrong, I tell myself as I complete a retainer agreement for a new matter at work, as I place cereal in my shopping cart at the grocery store, as I chop onions for the burritos we seem to have for dinner every other night. *Stop it*, I yell at myself. But I can't and the ball contracts a little more and the tears stream down my face. If Raymond sees me at this moment, I'll say it was the onions that made me cry.

If I wanted to, I could find a reason for these tears. After having a wonderful holiday together, Chris and I are disconnected again, snapping at each other and taking score over who is doing more for the family. I'm grateful for my flexible, part-time job but working for my father has its challenges. Michelle, my therapist, says it's unhealthy and keeps pushing me to find alternative work. I'm overwhelmed—trying to work, take care of the kids, get dinner on the table, and keep a clean house. My mother is slowly dying from lupus and pulmonary hypertension.

Pick a reason, any reason for the despair. But I know these

are all excuses. They are not the real causes of this emotional pain. It's just like how I used to justify my crying bouts when I was in my late twenties. After getting properly sloshed on whatever alcohol I had in my New York City apartment, I'd hole up in the bathroom with my drink and my Sony Walkman. I'd stare into the mirror and bawl over the deaths of my siblings while listening to emotional songs. I'm not saying that their deaths aren't tragic and sad. They are. But that's not why I was crying. That's the excuse I gave myself to drink and feel miserable.

"Poor me," they say in the meetings. "Pour me another drink."

I want to drink now. I know that it would make the tightness in my chest go away. I close my eyes and image the relief from the first long gulp of a vodka cranberry. The sting of the alcohol going down my throat would turn into a warmth that would radiate through my body, releasing the clench of my insides. The relief would be temporary, I know, but the desire to feel better, if even for only a couple of hours, is powerful.

I know I'm supposed to call someone. A newcomer. A sober sister. My sponsor. But Joy is just going to say I need to go to more meetings. And I don't want to go. She will say I need to get a sponsee. And I don't want a sponsee. She'll say that I need to be of service to someone else to stop thinking about myself, to let my higher power in.

I'm of service to everyone every day! I argue with her in my head. I make the kids breakfast, and then pack their lunches, then drive them to school, then go to work, where I'm called upon to help my mom. I pull on her compression socks and take her to the doctor. After work, I stop at the grocery store. Then I pick up the kids at school. I make them a snack, help with their homework, make dinner, clean up the kitchen, and then put them to bed. My entire day is being of service! But yet I still feel like crap. I feel like I want to die. I have visions of slashing my wrists.

Quick swipes of a razor producing thin red strips of blood. Not to kill myself but to release the pain that's stuck inside.

You are a mother, I scold myself. You shouldn't feel this way. My motherly love should overpower my chest-clenching sadness. But it doesn't and I feel guilty. At least I'm showing up for the day, when all I want to do is hide out in my closest, lying down in the dark next to the dormant running shoes and dust bunnies. My daily duties feel like Herculean accomplishments to me. Wiping peanut butter on bread and sticking it in a lunch box feels like I'm hiking a mountain. Throwing my hair up in a ponytail and putting on jeans to take them to school feels like I'm running a marathon. One day, I can't even put on jeans. All day long I stay in the sweatpants that I wore to bed.

How do other moms do it? When I pick Raymond up from school at 1:30 p.m. to take him to his allergist appointment, I feel like I'm supermom. *See, I'm doing it!* I want the world to take note. I'm doing it, even though I want to hide in the closet with a bottle of vodka. But the supermom feeling fades when the allergist asks the names of Ray's current medications, and I can't remember. I meant to write them down and bring them to the appointment, but I forgot.

Can't you see I'm doing the best I can?! I want to yell at the allergist, who turns away from us in his swivel chair to type something into Raymond's file on the computer. Probably something along the lines of: "Mother is a fuckup."

On my way to work the next day, I drive past an old Presbyterian church. Its huge red door is decorated with a wreath left over from Christmas. I have a strong urge to pull the car over and curl up on the stoop, like a homeless person. *Just leave me be. Just leave me to lay on this cold cement stoop.* I imagine the roughness of the cement on my cheek. I want to feel physically what I'm feeling emotionally. Hard, cold loneliness.

There is nothing wrong, I remind myself again. You have a nice house with a big backyard in a small town with three wonderful children and an understanding husband who wants to spend time with you, who helps out around the house after he works hard at his job. But the more I try to will the sadness away, the more the ball contracts, squeezing out tears.

On Saturday, the sadness hits me again in Ikea. I'm there to buy a desk for Julia's room. I volunteered for this task because it seemed like the lesser of two evils. It is easier to drive to the City of Elizabeth than to be around my kids with this chest-tightening and the sighing. Last night, I read Kay Thompson's *Eloise* to four-year-old Julia while tears streamed down my face. She asked what was wrong and I could only shake my head and wipe my tears with my sleeve. What psychological damage am I doing to my kids?

"My mom wept while she read books to me at night," Julia will tell her therapist.

On the way home, I'm driving past the oil refineries on the Turnpike when my cell phone rings. The minivan's screen tells me it's Alice. Alice had six months sober when I first came to the meetings and appeared to know everything about AA. I followed her around for weeks, literally mimicking her. Alice thanked the speakers, so I thanked the speakers. Alice gave her number to a newcomer, so I gave my number to newcomers. She had what I wanted: confidence and a lightness. So I did what she did.

For two seconds, my finger hovers above the screen between decline and accept. I don't want to talk to anyone in this state. I have nothing good to say. But I accept the call with a pang of regret. Through the Bluetooth speaker, she talks for a bit about her newborn son and then asks, "How are you?" I try to say I am fine, but the tears start to flow and I'm sobbing. I tell her about how I've been feeling. I tell her the truth.

"It's going to be all right," she says. Her calming voice is an immediate balm for my pain. It feels good to admit my sadness out loud to someone, to get it out of my head.

"Feelings aren't facts," she says. It's a dorky phrase but when she says it, it makes me smile. She is a kindergarten teacher and I feel like one of her snotty-faced students on the first day of school. I tell her that I'm not okay. That maybe I'm depressed. Like clinically depressed. She asks if I've talked to our sponsor Joy about this.

"No," I admit, which seems ridiculous when I say it aloud. *Why wouldn't I talk to the person who has vowed to help me?* Alice says that if I have to, I should seek outside help. By this, she means maybe I need to go back to my therapist. I had stopped seeing her when things seemed to be better.

"I'm afraid that Chris will think I've done something bad again if I tell him I need to go back to therapy." It wouldn't be unreasonable for him to think so; that's what happened two years ago.

"It's not your job to manage his feelings," Alice says to me, probably for the hundredth time.

After I finish the call with Alice, I call Joy. She picks up immediately, which she will do if she hasn't heard from me in a couple of days. I tell her what's been going on, how I've been sad all the time when there is really nothing wrong.

"Why am I still like this?" I whine at the microphone. "I should be better by now."

"Oh my God, Liz," she says. "We are not cured. There is no cure for alcoholism! We get a daily reprieve contingent on our spiritual condition," she says. "It says so right in the book: 'When these feeling crop up . . .' Not 'if,' but 'when.'"

Everything she says makes sense. I am always amazed that when I come to her with a real problem, she always gives the right advice. I'm surprised because she doesn't always have her shit together. She has told me more than once that she wants to punch her mother-in-law in the face, and I'm sure some doctor has noted her parental mistakes in a file. One time I commented on the fact that she always seems to say the right thing. She said it has nothing to do with her. That she prays for her higher power to speak through her. That sometimes she doesn't even remember what she said.

Now, as I drive in my minivan on the New Jersey Turnpike, with an Ikea desk clunking around in the back, she (or is it her higher power?) speaks to me through the car's speakers. Later, when I try to remember what exactly she said, I can't. But I know that she offered me absolution for my sadness. "We cannot control our feelings." And she gave me advice on what to do to stop feeling like this. A way to pull on the contracting ball so that I may feel better. A way to let my higher power in.

I'm almost to our exit, almost home, but I call Chris anyway. I tell him I need to go to a meeting tomorrow, the 8:30 a.m. beginners' meeting, so I can seek out new sponsees. The plastic ball trap around my chest expands and I can breathe.

MY NIGHTLY REVIEW IN THE MORNING

Step Eleven: Sought through prayer and meditation to improve our conscious contact with God as we understood Him, praying only for knowledge of His will for us and the power to carry that out.

March 2013
Two years sober

The steam from my coffee cup spirals up in the predawn darkness. It's 5:15 a.m., and Chris is next to me in bed, scrolling through news headlines on his phone. The house is perfectly still. The kids won't be up for another hour, when I'll need to start making their school lunches and getting them ready for the day. But right now, in this moment, I have time for my morning ritual. This is my favorite time of day. I cherish these quiet moments before sunrise.

A few months ago, our sober family gathered at my sober sister Jen's lovely home. My sponsor had asked her sponsor, Lynn, to come and talk to our group about Step Eleven. I'm not sure what precipitated this call to action. Maybe Lynn told Joy that she should be doing a nightly review. That's usually how we get information passed down. Joy's sponsor gives Joy direction about her sobriety, and Joy passes it on to us.

"It makes no sense to be in a twelve-step program and not be doing all the steps," my "grand-sponsor" declared to the group. We spilled out across the living room. A few people perched on stools; one person sat on an ottoman petting Jen's poodle. I sat on the couch, wedged between Alice and Jessica. We all nodded. Everything she said was making sense. She went on to explain Step Eleven and the purpose of the nightly review. She told Carrie to read the passage on the nightly review from the Big Book.

"Sure," Carrie said.

Beginning with, "Hi, I'm Carrie and I'm an alcoholic," she read: "When we retire at night, we constructively review our day. Were we resentful, selfish, dishonest, or afraid? Do we owe an apology?"[1]

Lynn went on to explain that we need nightly review partners, someone to hold us accountable. She instructed us to exchange the reviews with each other via email. This should be someone in our sober family, but not someone we are too close with. Not someone who is our good friend. Joy looked around the room and immediately paired us up. Jessica and I were assigned to each other. We smiled and waved at each other across the room.

I take my first sip of coffee (strong, just how I like it; *thank you, nighttime self, for setting it up*) and reach for my phone to pull up my nightly review questions. Jessica already emailed hers last night, because she's a good sober "doobie" who does her review at night like we're supposed to. But me? I'm unable to do the review at night. At night I feel brain-dead and tired and cranky. The morning is when I feel alive and ready to properly review. My brain is fresh now, caffeinated and clear, ready to look back on yesterday with honest eyes.

The bedside lamp casts a soft glow as I start typing my responses, checking each question carefully:

Did I pray? Yes, I whispered words this morning while waiting for the coffee to brew: "Please show me how I can be of service today." The words come naturally now, without the awkwardness they had in early sobriety, when prayer felt like speaking a foreign language.

Did I meditate? I smile and type "no," my perpetual answer. The morning light is starting to creep through our bedroom window. Maybe one day I'll be out there on our deck with a meditation cushion, but for now, this quiet morning review is my meditation.

I pause at "Was I resentful?" Yesterday floods back, that moment at the pharmacy, the sharp edge in someone's voice. It's still there, a small knot in my stomach. I type it out, watching the words appear on the screen. The knot loosens as I acknowledge it.

The questions continue, each one a flashlight illuminating corners of yesterday that I might have missed. Chris glances over at me from his phone, but I stay focused. This is my time with my higher power, my daily spiritual check-in.

When I get to "Was I kind and loving toward all?" I have to admit, about the pharmacy incident: "No, I had attitude right back." The truth doesn't sting like it used to. Progress, not perfection, right? I can hear the heat kick on downstairs, reminding me that soon I'll need to get up and start the day, with lunches to pack, kids to wake, breakfast to make.

I finish up with my gratitude list: "Grateful for: This quiet morning. Coffee. The ability to look at myself honestly without shame." I mean every word.

I hit send on my email to Jessica. Chris glances over and asks, "All done with your 'morning' nightly review?" He teases me about this reverse timing. I give him a playful nudge as I set my coffee cup on the nightstand. Pretty soon I'll need to head downstairs and start making sandwiches, but I feel it, that subtle shift that comes from starting my day in conscious contact with my higher power. I'm centered, grateful, and most importantly, sober. Another twenty-four hours stretches ahead, full of possibilities for service and growth.

This morning practice might not be what the Big Book authors had in mind when they wrote about the nightly review, but it works for me. Sometimes, being a rebel means finding your own path to the same destination. As long as I'm moving toward spiritual progress, I figure my higher power doesn't mind the timing.

SEEKING SPONSEES

Step Twelve: Having had a spiritual awakening as the result of these Steps, we tried to carry this message to alcoholics, and to practice these principles in all our affairs.

April 2013
Two years sober

At the Stone Church beginners' meeting on Saturday mornings, I reach out my hand to people who are "counting days," newcomers to AA who have less than ninety days of sobriety. Most of the time I say something like, "Wow, you look great! I was a sobbing snotty mess during my first ninety days," which isn't an exaggeration. When I ask for the newcomers' phone numbers and punch them into my phone's contact list, I usually put some designation so that I know this person is an AA person. I say "Jane Stone Church," which means I met this person at the Stone Church meeting. When I do this, I feel like I'm participating in some ancient AA ritual. I think about what it was like for people before cell phones. Everyone must have carried a pen and their "little black books" around with them. Usually, I immediately text the newcomer, so they have my phone number. "Hi, I'm Liz from (fill in the name of the meeting)." Back in the day, did people have to call each other on landlines? Did they call their sponsor from phone booths on the street?

On Sunday, I call three new people, but no one picks up. It happens that way sometimes. I'm not offended by it. On Monday night I go to the Candlelight Beginners' meeting, one of the first meetings I went to. And one that I used to lead. When the leader asks, "Is anyone counting days?" a woman raises her hand and says, "I was just released from the hospital. I have thirty days sober and need a sponsor." Immediately after the meeting, I go up to her and say, "I will be your sponsor." She nods and smiles and I tell her the deal. Call me every day. We will meet once a week to do "step work." I see some panic in her eyes at the mention of work, but I pat her hand and say, "You never have to feel this way again."

As the week progresses and I talk to my new sponsee on the phone every day and we make a plan to meet before home group, I can feel a lightness return. It feels like I've opened up the windows in my brain and let some fresh air in. The tasks that felt so heavy, like making the kids' lunches, return to their normal level. I don't love it, but I don't want to curl up in the closet with a bottle of vodka anymore.

When Joy sees me at the meeting and looks me in the eyes and says, "How are you doing?" I respond honestly. "Better, I'm doing better."

When, a few months later, my sponsee stops calling me and stops showing up to meetings, I express my frustration to Joy. She shrugs.

"Sponsees come and go, Liz. You are not their higher power. You can't get anyone sober. The important thing is that you didn't drink."

I see her point.

FIRE ON THE MOUNTAIN

> "If we are painstaking about this phase of our development, we will be amazed before we are halfway through. We are going to know a new freedom and a new happiness."
>
> —Ninth Step Promises, *Alcoholics Anonymous* [1]

March 17, 2012
One year and two months sober

I'm standing on the side of Okemo Mountain's bunny hill, optimistically called "Bright Star Basin." With my back to the slope-side condos, I'm watching two four-year-olds, my daughter Julia and Kelly and Scott's son Will, ride up the rubber "magic carpet" lift and then ski down the gentle slope. At the bottom, they automatically get back in line and do it again. They remind me of a toy I had as a kid: little plastic penguins continuously climbing up and sliding down a mountain.

It is nearing the end of the day and the sun has moved lower in the sky. Behind me, a newly born stream runs down the mountain. Winter is thawing. I close my eyes and tilt my head up towards the sun, welcoming the new season. When I open my eyes, I spot a large man skiing in a tartan kilt and a green shamrock T-shirt, holding a can of Guinness. It's St. Patrick's Day.

At this sight, my earlier contentment melts away like the snow and is replaced by an uncomfortable tug inside my gut and a twitch inside my brain. I'm angry that this man is drinking while skiing. It's ridiculous. Yet I'm jealous that he gets to drink when I can't. There's that alcoholic dichotomy again. It's unfair. And I'm annoyed that I feel all these conflicting emotions just because a guy is drinking a beer. I've been sober for over a year now. I want to feel normal. I want to be normal.

Now the sun feels too hot and I'm tired of standing awkwardly in my ski boots. When Julia and Will ski down the hill, I wave for them to come over. I'm ready for the day to end.

While I'm watching the four-year-olds, Chris is skiing with the older kids on the harder trails. We've been doing this ski weekend with Kelly and MaryBeth and their families every year since we graduated college. It's my second time attending sober, but this year feels different. The renewed connection between Chris and me is palpable—a far cry from last year, when we could barely look at each other.

On my first sober trip to Vermont, I had walked in on Chris in our guest bedroom, kneeling on the floor next to the bed, his head touching the bed's blue patchwork quilt, praying. I had turned around and walked out in disgust.

But now, on this St. Patrick's Day, it is two months past my one-year sober anniversary. I completed the Twelve Steps with my sponsor. I am a sponsor now, helping newcomers in the program.

The four-year-olds and I trek from the bunny slope over to the lodge. We dump our gear on a picnic table on the patio. The kids plead to take off their ski boots, and I give in. The staff buzzes around the patio, setting up a grill and rolling out kegs. There's the uncomfortable feeling again. The first beer after a day of skiing is true bliss, a reward for having schlepped around a mountain all day. The first gulp quenches the thirst and the second provides a warm glow that radiates from the stomach out to the limbs. It's a wonderful feeling I will never again get to experience.

On tap is a local Vermont brew, Magic Hat #9. *Can I still say it's my favorite beer even though I will never again drink it?* The band tunes up, a Grateful Dead cover band. I take stock of the scene. It's St. Patrick's Day, a holiday all about drinking. My favorite beer is on tap. I'm about to hear live music while sitting outside after skiing on a beautiful, springlike day in Vermont. It's my perfect storm, my ideal drinking scenario. The self-pity bubbles up inside of me and an invisible noose tightens around my neck.

"Think the drink through" is what I've been told to do in this situation. One pint of local brew on this patio will turn into three. By tonight, I'll be stealing vodka again. In two weeks, I'll drive drunk to pick the kids up from school. And my marriage will be over. The noose loosens its grip on me.

Of course, "Fire on the Mountain" is the band's first song. As the music fills the air, a warm glow grows within me. The kids dance in front of the band in their stocking feet. My sadness evaporates like their wet footprints on the stone patio. Instead of awkward, I'm content. Instead of jealous, I'm confident. Love swells inside me in the empty space where I used to pour vodka.

The late afternoon light is soft and the melting snow makes the air steamy. I scan the crowd of skiers coming off the mountain, looking for Chris. I spot him at the ski racks. He takes off his helmet and reveals a shock of gray hair. He turns, looks right at me, and grins. Time slows and my senses sharpen. I can hear every crisp note of the song and the steady whirring noise of the ski lifts. I can smell the hot chocolate and the melting snow. My vision becomes laser focused on Chris. He walks towards me, never dropping his gaze. Our love is a bright white electric current connecting us, like a rope tow pulling him to me. I stand motionless on the patio and the crowd around me vanishes. He reaches me and I rest my hand on his face and we kiss.

Later in the evening, when we are getting ready for bed, I ask him, "Did you feel that . . . connection?" I'm unsure how to name what happened between us.

"Of course," he says and hugs me. He has felt these moments before. It was me who was never present, who could not feel the love. I erected walls and insulated them with vodka, ensuring I wouldn't feel anything. The Twelve Steps lowered the walls. Draining the vodka made room for the love.

I lie in bed next to Chris, under the same blue patchwork quilt where he had prayed last year. Is this what he prayed for?

"Thank you," I whisper.

WHAT IT IS LIKE NOW

WHAT IT IS LIKE NOW
WHAT IT IS LIKE NOW
WHAT IT IS LIKE NOW
WHAT IT IS LIKE NOW

GRIEF IS LOVE

"Unable are the loved to die, for love is immortality."
—Emily Dickinson

February 2017
Six years sober

"And then there were three," my sister Roseann says to me.
"What?" I ask.

We are leaning up against the hospital walls, waiting for my father to say his last goodbyes to my mother, who minutes ago passed away. About a week ago, she got the flu and her immune-comprised body couldn't handle it. Ignoring her DNR wishes, we agreed to let the hospital put her on a ventilator. It was too difficult watching her gasp for breath. But after a day or two in the ICU and a conference with a palliative care doctor, it became clear she was not going to recover. At seventy-eight years old and after years of battling lupus, pulmonary hypertension, and COPD, she was ready to go and we were ready to let her. They removed the ventilator and switched her from the ICU to hospice. She died within hours.

"And then there were three," my sister Roseann repeats. "That should be the title of your memoir."

It isn't the right moment to explain to my sister that my memoir is about my recovery from alcoholism, not the tragic losses of our family. I remain silent.

After my dad says goodbye, we all walk out and down to the lobby. I think about the other times I have done this with my family. Waiting with my sisters for word from my parents about whether William was dead or alive. Driving home from the hospital with Roseann after we watched our sister Julia die. We each drove our own cars this time, so we say goodbye in the lobby. It is late, almost ten o'clock, but I call Alice on the way home from the hospital. I'm mostly confident I'm not going to stop at a liquor store on the way home, but why risk it. Alice keeps me company for the ten-minute ride.

The loss feels immense. Not only is it the loss of my mother, but she also takes with her part of my brother William and my sister Julia. My mom's loss unearths the buried grief of my siblings. I am devastated and spend a long time walking around in a daze. But I don't feel the need to drink, which seems like a miracle in itself. And I do all the things that I've done before that now are habit: I call Joy and the other women in my network, I go to my meetings and reach out my hand to newcomers. I pray to a god of my understanding.

I feel the loss, deeply and profoundly. This is the first time I've dealt with this kind of loss without a drink in my hand. I'm feeling all the feelings. My mother's favorite wildflower blooms and I sit down in the dirt and cry with my head in my hands. The loss hurts, but also, the hurt feels good? It's difficult to explain and the first time I try to explain I do it from the podium at an AA meeting.

I explain that for my sister's and brother's deaths I was so terrified of the pain of their loss that I drank away all the feelings. With my mother's death, alcohol is no longer a solution. So I am forced to feel all the feelings. And as I experience them,

I realize I am grateful for the feelings? My voice raises into a question because I'm still not sure and I'm not articulating it correctly. Because I am missing my mom, it means that I loved my mom. And love to me is my higher power. So grief equals love equals my higher power. It's a concept I still have trouble explaining.

Grief is love and even though loss is painful, I am so grateful to be able to feel that love, experience that love, and be present for it. I look up to see if this is resonating with anyone and I see several heads nod.

"Thank you for letting me share," I conclude.

FIRE ISLAND REVISITED

August 2019
Eight years sober

"Are you ready?" I ask Chris. We are on Fire Island, which has now become a yearly pilgrimage and includes all of Chris's family. We are about to embark on what has become an annual tradition: ride our bikes into the town of Ocean Beach, grab a latte at Rachel's, and then cruise around and try to identify all the houses we have rented over the years.

It's easy for me to know how many years we've been coming to Fire Island because it's one more than I've been sober. If I've been sober eight years then I know I've been coming to Fire Island for nine years. There was that one year. Our first year on Fire Island when, in addition to the Mike's Hard Lemonades I was drinking, I took swigs of the vodka the previous renter had left. I took swigs before I called Bob on the phone.

And whatever happened to Bob? Did his wife ever find out? Was he a serial adulterer or was I his one and only foray? I don't know. I will admit that in the beginning I would wonder. I would imagine what I would say to him if I ever ran into him. But I've long since washed my hands of the whole mess. And I've come to terms with the fact that the affair needed to happen. I wasn't going to get sober without it. I've learned to accept that the affair was a necessary step in my recovery. It was a trap door I constructed to escape from my alcoholic condition.

Chris loves riding his bike around Fire Island. I enjoy it too, as long as it doesn't turn into an epic thirty-mile bike ride, like the one we took on our honeymoon. I ride my bike with him because I know he likes it. He keeps it short because he knows I don't like long rides. We compromise now without having to discuss it or shout at each other about our various needs. After seventeen years of marriage, we know our needs.

When Chris is finally ready, we take off. I follow behind as he likes to lead. Our first stop is the small white ranch house with the big deck. It's the one where I called Bob, drunk, from the back deck while Chris was at the beach with the kids. But we don't mention that. There's no need to linger on those hurtful moments. We've spent too much time already doing that. The next stop is around the corner, a clapboard with green window frames and a screened-in front porch. This one is was a little too close to town but we still liked it. It was the first house we rented after I got sober, the house where I walked in and saw the Grey Goose glistening on the counter and ran outside to Chris, looking wild and panicky. I paced in front of this house while on the phone with Joy, who got Alice to find a meeting for me. Why I couldn't do this myself I don't know. But to this day I'm forever grateful for Alice's quick action and support.

We gaze on this house and sip our lattes. We look back on this memory fondly; it was a different time. It was also the trip on which Chris dislocated his shoulder and I got to show up for him, clear-eyed, clear-headed, and supportive. I can be those things when I don't have vodka coursing through my veins. We look at the next house and then the next. That's the house where we found that iPad in the couch cushion. There's the house my dad rented the one year he came out. The house our family friends, the Glovers, rented. Finally, we cruise back to our current house, one graciously rented for the extended Jannuzzi family by my sister-in-law Angela. Despite our lattes, we are tired, and while the kids decide to go on a bike ride into town, we take a nap.

ANY GIVEN NIGHT (IN THE PRESENT)

The mood in the living room is peaceful. The five of us, me, Chris, Michael, Ray, and Julia, are sprawled out on our sectional couch, watching *Modern Family* on the TV above the fireplace. We've just finished eating dinner and Chris and I have mostly cleaned up the dishes. Soon the kids will disperse to do homework, to play Fortnight, to Snapchat with their friends, but for this moment we are all here together.

"Is there anything for dessert?" Julia asks.

"Yes!" I reply. "I got ice cream today."

The three kids jump up and scramble into the kitchen, jokingly pushing each other out of the way. For a minute I can see them again as the young children they once were. I smile at their playfulness.

I glance at the clock on the cable box. It's 7:50 p.m. on Wednesday. Time to go to home group. The meeting that, years ago, my sponsor insisted I attend every week. The one for which I had to ask Chris to switch his studio night so he can be home with the kids while I attend the meeting. And I do attend it, week after week, month after month, year after year, missing it only rarely, for a vacation or a sick child. The meeting at which most everyone knows me, like a weird twist on the TV show about the neighborhood bar Cheers.

Where everybody knows your name.
And they're always glad you came.

When I was drinking, no one ever knew my name at the liquor store, because I would rotate which one I would go to for fear the store clerks would recognize me as an alcoholic buying vodka day after day. One day I would go to Vingo, near the car wash. The next day I would go to Spirits, in the grocery store shopping plaza. The following day I would go to a different Spirits in a town ten minutes away. Now I go to the same place week after week, where people do know my name, I am welcomed, and I'm most definitely recognized as an alcoholic.

I can leave my house so close to the start of the eight o'clock meeting because the parish house where the meeting is held is about a two-minute drive from my house. In 2014, we moved from the tiny, blue and white Cape to a larger house with a huge backyard, in a town with a better school system. It's the same town my sponsor lives in, and I bump into her on walks around the neighborhood.

I peel myself off the couch and run upstairs to wash my face and brush my teeth. Pulling my hair back into a ponytail, I glance at my face in the mirror. I'm fine with how I look. No need to gussy myself up. This is me. And I'm comfortable going to this meeting as me.

I bounce down the stairs and grab my purse and then stand behind the couch.

You'd think I wouldn't want to leave this scene. All of us together in one spot, comfortable on the couch, laughing easily at the jokes from a TV sitcom we all relate to. But now is when I feel like I can leave: when Chris and all three kids are content. They are fed. They are safe. They are happy. I'm not needed here. I can go.

"Ok, I'm heading to my meeting," I say to the backs of their heads.

Chris pulls his eyes away from the TV to glance at me. "Have a good meeting," he says with his classic wide Chris smile. The one that warms my heart. The one that lets me know he is in a good place, we are in a good place. This happiness comes so easily to him, and I long to be more like him. To so easily exude such a casual gratefulness. To so easily lean towards happiness. This meeting helps me with that. Without AA meetings, I don't have a strong sober network. Without a strong sober network, I do not have a connection to my higher power. Without a connection to my higher power, I cannot be of service to anyone else, and I quickly slide down into a depression. The meetings give me a rope to pull myself out of my self-pity spiral. When I climb out, Chris is there waiting for me with open arms and a quizzical look that asks: *Where have you been? Join me in this happy life.*

Without looking up from their phones, the kids say in unison, "Have a good meeting, Mom!" Something about the acknowledgment of "mom" warms my heart. They are talking to me as a person. Not "I want this" or "I need that." The way they emphasize "mom" implies, *Go ahead, Mom. You deserve this moment. Go have fun with your friends.*

Having their mother attend an Alcoholics Anonymous meeting is no big deal to my children. It's something they grew up with, something I always talk openly about. I imagine them telling their friends, "My mom? Yeah, she's an alcoholic. She goes to meetings all the time." This is my goal: to stop the cycle of shame and guilt caused by this family disease. No one should hide the fact that they suffer from a disease. I spent so many years hiding this shameful piece of me, this shameful piece of my family. It is such a relief to have it out in the open. By acknowledging my disease, I'm stripping it of its power.

I jump in the car and make the ridiculously short drive. It's only a mile! I could walk, I should walk, but I have only walked to home group once, when there was a snowstorm. I drive to the end of my street, make a right, and then I'm there.

There is a dirt parking lot behind the parish house, but it's always packed full, and I hate getting wedged in there. Instead, I turn right and park on a side street. The side street has tall brick columns that remind me of the movie *Back to the Future*, when Marty McFly, Michael J. Fox's character, goes back in time and sees his family's housing development in the fifties, before it was fully built up and grown in with trees and bushes. I prefer the grown-in version. The version that's been around for a while.

The side street has several parked cars on it. I'm not the only one who parks here to avoid the crowded parking lot. I wonder what the neighbors think. Do they ask: *What is going on at the church every Wednesday night between 7:15 and 9:15 p.m.?* Or maybe they know it's an AA meeting and they don't care.

A couple of years ago there was a controversy in our town about a new recovery center opening near our elementary school. The discussion on our town's Facebook group was heated. Opponents didn't want our kids to walk past the recovery center on the way to school. God forbid the kids see a drunk or addict. *Outside of their own home*, I said in my head, with an eye roll. Luckily I stayed out of the discussion on Facebook, but inwardly I seethed. I wanted to tell them all, "Do you know how many Twelve-Step meetings are going on around you at any given time? I attend a meeting in a building where a preschool meets at the same time! When they were young, I brought my kids to AA meetings. It's good for our kids to see that this is where people go to get help." The controversy came and went and the recovery center continues to operate in our town, near the school, without an issue. And by keeping my mouth shut I didn't cause a rift with the neighbors.

I exit the car and step into the summer night. Immediately my body and mind relax. I take in a deep breath. The summer night is full of the promise of expectation. Back in the day, in my teen years and early twenties, a summer night meant that ahead of me was a night of drinking and revelry. The "anything can happen" type of night that might end on the beach or at the police station.

Now the summer night is calming. I feel the night air seep into my pores. I cross the street but slow my gait; I don't want to enter the door to the meeting yet. I want to savor the moment. I pass two home group members sitting on the stoop of the church having a cigarette.

"Good evening, ladies!"

"Hello, Liz," they respond.

I love this. This easy, friendly transaction. I don't think, *Why am I not included in this tête-à-tête?* as maybe I would have in the past. I acknowledge they are close friends enjoying a moment and a last cigarette before they head into the meeting.

I pause a minute before climbing the cement steps to the back door. Right behind the door are greeters, two or three people whose commitment it is to say hello to me and make me feel welcome. I have a commitment too. For six months, I'm the person newcomers should go to if they are looking for a sponsor.

"If you need a sponsor, please see Liz," the leader states at the beginning of the meeting, and I stand up and wave so all the newcomers know who I am. So far, no one has taken me up on the offer, but I'm willing to help. "The willingness," Joy says, "will keep you sober."

Inside the door, the parish house will be crowded; my home group has gotten very popular over the last few years. Most people will be milling about chatting, getting a cup of coffee and cookies. There will be a few people there who will be dejected, slumped down in their chairs, wondering why everyone else is smiling and laughing when they can't drink anymore. At the end of the meeting, we will approach those newcomers, get their numbers, and tell them, "You never have to feel this way again."

My close friends, Alice, Mary, and Joy, are all inside. I have an easy rapport with these women and feel so comfortable around them. They know all of me, the good and the bad.

With one foot on the cement step, I breathe in. I continue to savor this feeling, this suspended moment on the cusp of a promise. A promise that everything is going to be okay. And it is, for today.

If you are struggling with alcohol or addiction, AA can help. Visit aa.org to find a meeting near you.

THE APPENDIX—MY PODIUM STORY

Transcribed from a recording on August 31, 2022
Eleven years, seven months, twenty-three days sober

Hi. I'm Liz. I'm an alcoholic. My sober date is January 8th, 2011. My sponsor is Joy, she has a sponsor, etc. I've sponsored women in the past but currently do not have any sponsees and I'm available for sponsorship. My home group is Fort Monmouth Wednesday night in West Long Branch at 8:00 p.m.

So the first time I got drunk was in eighth grade. I'm the youngest of four, and all my older siblings drank. I'm from a large extended family and there was always alcohol present at family events. In fact, I remember being surprised when I went to another family's house for dinner that there wasn't a long cocktail hour. At age thirteen, I wanted to see what this drinking thing was all about. So I stole alcohol from my parents and from the people I [babysat] for, a gross mix of vermouth and scotch, and I mixed it in a Ball jar. I hid the Ball jar in a trunk in my room until our eighth grade overnight trip to Washington, DC. I wrapped the Ball jar in socks and put it in my overnight bag. The stealing and the hiding foreshadowing how I would end up drinking. I shared a room with three other girls. I passed around that Ball jar and we all took sips and got silly. But I was the only one who drank so much that I actually vomited and was hung over the next day, for the rest of the tours of DC.

But being hung over didn't stop me. I enjoyed the feeling of the buzz. And I chased the buzz. Partying was the thing to do in my suburban New Jersey town. As I headed into high school, I was all about the party. I surrounded myself with other people who drank the way I drank. Every weekend, we'd figure out whose parents were away and how we were going to get alcohol.

As I was starting my drinking career, my older brother, William, he was four years older than me, he was getting in trouble for his drinking. He had an accident and got in trouble with police. My parents sent him to a boarding school to get him away from "the wrong crowd" (meanwhile *he* was the wrong crowd). And when he got kicked out of boarding school, they sent him to rehab and then another rehab. When he was in rehab, we were forced to go to family therapy sessions and my sister and I had to go to an Al-Anon meeting. Because of this, I knew what it meant to be an alcoholic. I knew it was a disease. We had those pamphlets at home that asked the questions: Do you drink before you go out? Do you black out often? Even at age sixteen and seventeen, all my answers were yes. So I knew, even though I surrounded myself with other partiers, I knew that I drank differently from them. I knew that I was an alcoholic like my brother.

But . . . I didn't want to stop drinking. I knew if I could stay under the radar, no one would call me out on my drinking and no one would tell me I had to stop. I did my best to try to control it, and to hide it. Even still, there were many moments [when] I woke up filled with guilt, shame, and remorse [about] what I could remember [from] the night before. The way I handled those negative feelings was to drink over them. Stuff it down and move on to the next party.

I get through high school and the summer after I graduated, my brother William, who had been sober for three years but had relapsed and moved back home, went out to a party, and drove home drunk and died in a car accident. I was eighteen. This was obviously a very tragic moment for my family, but never once did I see how alcohol or alcoholism played a part in my brother's death. I always chalked it up to my brother being a wild guy. I didn't stop drinking and I didn't think twice about my own drinking. In fact, I drank more to wash away my grief.

Next, I go off to college, and college is more of the same. A lot of partying. People often talk about how they go to college and start drinking more. I actually drank less when I first went to college because I didn't immediately find my people. Then I ended up getting a boyfriend at a fraternity house and I was able to once again surround myself with other people who drank like me: fraternity brothers. There'd be shots of Jäger at every party.

College is more of the same. Lots of partying; moments of guilt, shame, and remorse. I'd call the day after a particular crazy night "a baseball hat day," because I'd wear my baseball hat covering my face because I was too ashamed to look at anybody in the eyes.

I make it through college okay. And I am back at home in New Jersey, trying to start my career and my life, when tragedy number two happens to my family. My older sister Julia dies by suicide. I am already drinking so much that I don't even know if I process any of that grief. And I've been through this before and I know [how] to handle it: I just drink more.

I move to New York City, and I'm living with a roommate. At this point, it's not so cool anymore to drink as much as I had been drinking. It's starting to get scary in the city to be blackout drunk, walking around the streets of Hell's Kitchen a drunken mess; it's not safe. I'm also silently dealing with the grief of losing my sister. What I end up doing more and more at that time is drinking by myself. It's like I discovered a new way to drink: I don't have to go to the bars or some party; I can do this by myself. I love it when my roommate is gone for the night. I get a six pack of beer or Mike's Hard Lemonade, and a pack of cigarettes. I take my drink and my cigs and my yellow Sony Walkman, and I go into the bathroom, stare at myself in the mirror, and cry and drink and smoke and cry some more. That's how I spend a Friday night as a young twenty-five-year-old in the Greatest City in the World.

And it's hard to explain, but that's how *I had* to spend a Friday night. Like I had to do that in order to make it through the week. I had to have those nights by myself to drink the way I wanted to drink, until I totally passed out, in order to function as a regular human in my job and socially with friends.

I meet my husband at work, and we start dating. My higher power was watching out for me then and I fell in love with someone who doesn't like to drink. When we were dating, we'd go out to bars, and after one or two drinks, he'd be like, "Okay, let's go." And I'd be like, *What? I'm just getting started.* He's sipping his first Maker's Mark and I've downed two vodka gimlets and want to hit a third. But to tell him I want to have another drink would be to admit I had a drinking problem, and I still know I need to hide the way I drink from everyone. Especially because of what happened with my brother and sister. I'm not like them. I'm fine. Everything is fine. Don't look over here at my drinking.

I'm married now and it's my honeymoon. We get a gift basket from our coworkers with a huge bottle of champagne. I want to hang out and drink the champagne and Chris wants to go on a thirty-mile bike ride. It's at that moment that I realize the pickle I'm in. How am I going to drink the way I want to drink while living with this guy? So, from the beginning of our marriage, I start to push him away. I encourage him to go out with his friends. You want to go sailing for the night? Go. Sure. You want to go jam at the studio? Go. And he does. And I have my nights to myself. While he's out doing his thing, I'm at home drinking the way I want to drink, so I can still have those nights where I stare in the mirror with my Sony Walkman and cry and drink and he still doesn't know about it.

We have three children. I do believe my progression would have been faster if I didn't have children because I was able to stop drinking (for the most part) when I was pregnant. I might have had a beer or two here and there, but I was not drinking alcoholically. Between each pregnancy, when I would stop nursing and my alcoholism would start to progress, I'd drink more and more. And then I'd get pregnant again and I'd stop drinking for the moment. I was able to control it during that time.

But then I had my third child, my daughter Julia, and I can remember the moment [when] I made the decision to not hold back anymore. My husband Chris was away visiting his family with the younger two and I was with my son Michael, who was five at the time. We had a really difficult day. And the way I dealt with it is, I stopped at a liquor store and picked up a bottle of vodka. I knew at that point [that] by making that decision, to buy vodka instead of Mike's Hard Lemonade or beer, I was making the decision that this isn't about just relaxing with a drink. I chose vodka so you wouldn't smell it on me, so I [could] drink a lot without feeling full. Not consciously, but at that moment, I made a decision for alcohol to be my solution.

This wasn't the first time I clearly chose alcohol. In high school, when I was a sophomore, I was treated for depression. I went to my mom and I told her how bad I was feeling and she got me help. I went to a psychiatrist, and I was prescribed psychotropic medication, and it worked. But the doctor warned I couldn't drink on the medication. And I wanted to go to a Grateful Dead concert and drink. So I weaned myself off the medication. And from that point on, alcohol became my way to conquer my problems. For me, when I take a sip of vodka, it's like a thick coat of paint, smoothing out all my imperfections and cracks. I feel brand new. It's what I use for my depression, for my grief, for any anxiety. I used alcohol to get through life.

From that point on, my progression goes fast. I drink during the day while I am home watching the kids. There were times when I drank and drove with them in the car. I would always start the day saying I wasn't going to drink too much. Or I'm going to wait until the kids go to bed. But then I'd find myself drinking after the second cup of coffee in the morning. I'd wake up feeling like shit; by 10:00 a.m. I would start thinking, *You know what would make me feel better?*

I would have this routine when Chris was away, traveling on a business trip. I would do something with the kids that would make me feel like a good mother, like take them to the Great Adventure Safari or the park, and then on the way home I'd swing by McDonald's and then, while they were munching on french fries, I would go to the liquor store. I'm able to hide this routine from Chris because he travels a lot. Also, apparently, I'm a good liar, which I didn't realize until I came to AA and really looked at my behavior. So Chris, he has no idea. And I'm doing like crazy things, like having the one bottle on display while there's other bottles behind it that I'm drinking out of, or throwing out vodka bottles in the garbage, only to retrieve them later.

So anyway, my drinking gets worse. My life at this point is miserable. I don't know how to fix it. I know that the drinking is causing a problem, but I also know I cannot live without alcohol. I couldn't survive without drinking. Things between my husband and me are really bad. And then it all comes to a head in one terrific, horrible fight where both of us reveal some bad things we had done in the marriage.

And I could have just let it stay there, just have that horrible fight, and we probably would have gotten a divorce. But in the moment, when we were revealing the bad things we had done, I also revealed how much I was drinking. That I was drinking vodka during the day while watching the kids. When the words come out of my mouth, I can tell you I wanted to shove them back in because I knew what that meant. I knew [that] the minute I said the words to him, I could no longer drink.

Chris was relieved. He had known something was not right with his wife and our marriage, but he didn't know what or how to fix it. So, me finally admitting that I was drinking was a relief to him.

Once I said the words, I knew I had to stop drinking. I was seeing a therapist at the time and she recommended I see an [alcoholism] therapist, who of course told me I had to go to an AA meeting. I went to the Thursday night Women's Step meeting and immediately met wonderful women, who surrounded me and told me I never had to feel that way again.

I went to one meeting a week and felt better during the meeting, but then I'd have to go home to my house, where things between me and Chris were really really bad. I didn't understand why. I had stopped drinking, I was going to a meeting; why weren't things getting better? The women kept telling me I had to go to other meetings, I had to get a home group, I had to find a sponsor. I hung on for a while going to one meeting a week, and I made it through Christmas and New Year's Eve without drinking. And then something happened after the Christmas break. My husband went back to work and the kids went to school, I sat at home by myself, and I drank. After that, I realized I needed to really embrace the program more.

I started doing what the women suggested, and I went to their meetings, and that's where I met my sponsor, Joy. She got me working the steps immediately. As I said, at that time, my life was a shitshow. My marriage was falling apart and I couldn't fix it. I was so grateful to try something like the Twelve Steps just to have something to do. I had the gift of desperation.

I remember reading the "Ninth Step Promises" lying in bed one night with Chris; I don't think he was talking to me at the time, but I was trying to patch things up and I was like, "Listen to all these promises. This book says all this will come true if we work the steps. Can you believe it?" He continued to ignore me. Even though at that time I thought, *no way is this program going to do all these things for me*, I can tell you now that all those promises came true in my life.

I went through the steps with Joy. Some were easier than others. I could admit I was alcoholic. However, I had trouble admitting [that] my life was unmanageable, which is ridiculous in hindsight. But even as I was drinking vodka during the day, I maintained a job, I was raising the kids, I had a house and a car and hadn't gotten a DWI, although I should have. I didn't realize how unmanageable my life was—lying to my husband, drinking while taking care of the kids—until I wrote it all out in black and white.

Regarding the Third Step. I grew up Catholic. I majored in religious studies in college, so I've always been seeking some sort of spirituality. I had some trouble with the "Everything is God's will" concept. In the beginning, I refused to believe it was God's will to have my sister Julia die by suicide. [Voice shakes, eyes get teary.] It's been twenty-five years and this is still how I react. Anyway, I was able to come to terms with that. I was able to see [that] Julia was suffering and perhaps her death was God's will to end her pain. And that's how I came to accept a God of my understanding. It's not the Catholic God I grew up with. It's more of a general spirit. I use nature a lot as my higher power. I enjoy being out in the woods or at the ocean.

Steps Four and Five were amazing. At first you think, how is writing down my resentments going to help? I'm just getting pissed off at the world all over again. But going through it with my sponsor, Joy, and seeing my part in my resentments was so eye-opening. Steps Six and Seven—I was happy to see that a lot of what had happened was my part, because that meant I could work on fixing it. If you're constantly blaming everybody else, you know, there's nothing you can do about that. But it was empowering to me to realize that I could fix my own problems. Steps Eight and Nine were very healing. I was able to make amends to my husband. It was a very healing moment. He was also in Al-Anon, so he was working the steps with [his] sponsor, and he made his amends to me.

It didn't feel fast at the time, but I can tell you in hindsight we healed our marriage very quickly. It was December 2010 when my marriage fell apart, and by October 2011, we renewed our vows on our ten-year wedding anniversary. We recommitted to our marriage and now have been married twenty years. Our marriage is so much stronger from the hell we went through.

So, one last thing I should end with. The way I used to grieve was to drink over it. That's how I dealt with the loss of my brother and my sister. So, when my mother died five years ago, I was able to experience her death sober. It was sad but also so beautiful. Grief is love and even though loss is painful, I was so grateful to be able to feel that love, experience that love, and be present for it.

That's all I have for now. Thank you for listening.

ACKNOWLEDGMENTS

My gratitude bucket runneth over. Where to begin? Perhaps with a special thanks to Corinne LeBaron. Because of her post on Facebook in 2015, I discovered Project Write Now, a wonderful nonprofit writing organization based out of Red Bank, NJ. Thank you to PWN's instructors for helping me put words on a page, and to book inc, its spin-off department, for getting me to assemble those snippets into an actual book. I'm grateful to all the writers I've met through classes, conferences, and retreats who've encouraged me and, more importantly, kvetched with me during this roller-coaster writing journey. And thank you to Brooke Warner for the green light to publish, and to the entire team at She Writes Press for turning my manuscript into an actual book!

I'm deeply grateful to my extended family and long-term friends who have been with me since before sobriety, loving me despite my disease. Kelly, you deserve a special shout-out for not only being there through it all, God bless you, but also being my first nonwriter reader who said, "Yes, I like it. It's good." Though I know you would've said that regardless.

To my father, who encouraged my writing from college onward with a never-ending subscription to the *New Yorker.* To my mother, who, even on her deathbed, unable to speak due to her tracheostomy tube, motioned with arthritic hands for me to keep writing. And to my sister Roseann—perhaps the only person who truly knows what it's like to be in my shoes, having also lost a brother, sister, and mother—thank you for your continuous support!

To "The Firm" (our family group chat)—Chris, Michael, Raymond, and Julia. You are my heart, my everything. Kids, I love how you respond with genuine enthusiasm to my writing achievements: "That's great, Mom. Good for you." It melts my heart. And Kristoff, when I offered you veto power over *Sober Mom*, you said: "I'm so proud of you. Why would I want to get in the way of your dreams?" Thank you, thank you, thank you.

The bottom line is this: I never could have written any book—especially one about recovery—if I were still drinking. I tried writing as an active alcoholic and failed spectacularly. (Once, I dropped out of an online writing class after spilling a screwdriver and frying my keyboard.) Being a published writer had been my dream since I was a child, but before I could become one, I had to remove the alcohol from my mind, body, and spirit. For my sobriety, I'm indebted to those wonderful reformed drunks who share their experience, strength, and hope. Especially my sponsor, who guided me through the Twelve Steps, which "rocketed me to the fourth dimension," and those women—God, those women—I'm crying now as I write this—who circled around me at that first meeting saying, "You never have to feel this way again." This book wouldn't exist without your tireless support. I'm so grateful to be trudging the road to happy destiny with you.

Now, let's have some cake and coffee!

ENDNOTES

Prologue

1 Some names and identifying characteristics have been changed to protect a person's identity.

A Word on AA's Eleventh Tradition

1 Alcoholics Anonymous General Service Office

When a Man Loves a Woman

1 "More About Alcoholism," *Alcoholics Anonymous*, p. 43.

Finding a Sponsor

1 *Alcoholics Anonymous Comes of Age*, p. 279.

Finding My Higher Power

1 At this time I still said "commit suicide." After being educated that the word "commit" stigmatizes suicide, I've since changed to "die by suicide."

Fire Island

1 *Alcoholics Anonymous*, p. 164.

My Nightly Review in the Morning

1 *Alcoholics Anonymous*, p. 86.

Fire on the Mountain

1 "Ninth Step Promises," *Alcoholics Anonymous*, p. 83-84.

ABOUT THE AUTHOR

Author photo © Danny Delucia of DeLucia Digital

Elizabeth Jannuzzi writes about loss, motherhood, and recovery from alcoholism. Her essays have appeared in *HuffPost, The Rumpus, Under the Gum Tree, Memoir Monday, Brevity Blog*, and elsewhere. She earned a Best of the Net nomination in 2023 and serves as program director at Project Write Now, a nonprofit writing organization. Elizabeth lives in Shrewsbury, NJ with her husband and writes a weekly Substack newsletter on recovery. Visit www.elizabethjannuzzi.com.